ONE WITH GOD

ONE WITH GOD:

Awakening Through the Voice of the Holy Spirit

Book 7

Marjorie Tyler
Joann Sjolander
Margaret Ballonoff

One With God:
Awakening Through the Voice of the Holy Spirit
Book 7

ISBN: 978-0-578-32918-5
Library of Congress Control Number: 2021922082

Cover and text design: Vanimdesign.com

Sacred Life Publishers™
SacredLife.com
Printed in the United States of America

Foreword

What do You say, Holy Spirit?

It is important to recognize that you are still caught in the phenomenal world of form. Images yet hold power for you and are compelling, not unlike a series you enjoy on Netflix. You believe you are operating with a fully awakened mind but you are not. You are stuck in the world of dreams, holding to My promise of an experience completely outside the dream. That will happen in the "near" future; near in relation to having lived eons asleep. You are on the edge of waking, like the painting often ascribed to Giordano Bruno that shows a man peering through the edge of the world into infinity; coming out of a dream.

You cannot rush the trajectory of awakening that I have set for you, though it is becoming clearer by the day. Both Jo and Meera are having experiences of seeing form turn into "waves of energy" indicating that form is not solid. You are not your bodies and each of you grasp that concept. This is where I want you at this point of our journey Home. You do not need to hurry it up. Know that I am leading you slowly, step-by-step, and you are right where I want you.

The world of form must be enough of a "reality" for you to accomplish your mission, which right now is putting Book 7 into the world. I have manifested that from a thought that was concurrent with your "birth" into a phenomenal world. You must paint the picture and write the story of the awakening of mind to Me as your Only Reality. This is why you are so drawn to "Bruno's" vision. It was a foreshadowing of what you have come to understand thus far, and is enough for now. Let the rest unfold. You *will* go beyond form, but that is not where I want your focus.

Book 7 brings the readers to their own point of taking the last steps into Unity as One with God. Celebrate this threshold.

Book 8 will give a picture of a completed mission. Take the time to savor the details of your life given to Me. We are One and are watching the story from beyond the battleground—right at the edge of a made-up planet called Earth.

1

A Team of One

I am not a separate entity named "Holy Spirit" who resides in your head.

April 22, 2017

Holy Spirit, please control my mind. I do manage your mind because you have given it to Me. This has allowed you to recognize the ego, especially when it surreptitiously pops up. As you open only to My Thoughts, the ego is silenced. We go this day together as One Mind. You like that thought and it seems new. Until now, you have seen Me as a separate mind—independent from your chattering ego thought system, but I am not a separate entity named "Holy Spirit" who resides in your head. I am your Christ Self in the Mind of God. That thought is overwhelming, almost more than you are willing to accept. The truth is that you are the Mind and Thought of God—One with Him. We are coming to the point where I will rule your whole mind. Your ego is already slinking away because it knows it has been beaten. You have chosen Me as the only one on your team; the only Player, so I have "won the game." You no longer are playing against your Self.

The ego was mt's default, always in the background; an automatic member of the team. But there is no longer any team; no longer anything to choose. You have made the only choice there is to make and I am it. Be Still and Know that I AM God. This, you now receive without question. *Holy Spirit, can I still ask You questions?* Yes. The part of you that "asks" is the part not yet fully awake. Soon there will be no need to ask because you will

Know. The awareness of My Will as your will becomes natural; simultaneous.

There is still a lingering "sense of separation" between us, which is why you still supplicate Me. That will soon disappear and your thoughts will be directly My Thoughts without an intermediary. You now think of all the priests and gurus who have taken on the role of being the "one mind." Humanity gave away its power to the external world of substitutes for Me, for God. You are done with substitutions. There is only One Life. I am the Answer and I am the question. *How can You be the question if You are always the Answer?* Every Answer contains the implicit question of "who am I?" I am the Answer to everything. My Answer is ready at every turn of the road. You accept what I am telling you now, which is all that is needed for you to know that you will reach God in this lifetime.

2

The Stimulus

The dream of separation was essential for the expansion of the mind of the One Son.

April 28, 2017

The "you" I speak to is the you in the mind who knows your reality as Me—your Self. We refer to it as the decision maker (DM)—the part of the mind that chose to try out an independent life and has now chosen to awaken. The DM knew it was Home but chose to delude "itself" until this point in the dream cycle. It always had the capacity to see the truth and is the part of you that placed you on the path Home. Of course, you guessed it . . . that part is Me, the Holy Spirit.

Now I am confused. You are saying that the decision maker, which chose the separation, is also the part that chose the return and it has always been You? Yes, I am it all. I am the Decision Maker. I am your Whole Mind. I am the Memory of God. I am the Stimulus to find one's life outside of the Kingdom and then return to the Kingdom. This dream of separation was essential for the expansion of the mind of the One Son of God who "fell asleep and who will awaken." It is no different from the story of Jesus, born of woman, living in the world, dying in the world, then rising above the world. This is the experience each dream character will undergo, yet none of those experiences are real. They are just representations of the "one tiny thought of separation" that will collapse in the moment of awakening. This is becoming clearer day by day. Remember that the separation lasted less than a nanosecond and was immediately Corrected by Me. We are just reviewing a dream made up in the sleeping mind. That dream is now evaporating.

3

Seeds of God

It only takes one of you for the Light to surge throughout the mind.

April 29, 2017

I gave you a dream in the early morning hours to specifically reflect what you are now experiencing in your earth life. It was late spring and you were looking at your garden. There was a lot of greenery but clearly no flowers. You long for flowers and were chastising yourself for not having planted any seeds. Now it was too late to have a crop. You then remembered you had started seedlings in small flats in your cellar, like in your childhood home. Because they were planted so long ago, perhaps months, you couldn't recall anything about them. Even though you figured they all must be dead, you went down and uncovered the containers. Miraculously, you discovered that each little cell had burgeoned with deep green sprouts. They were strong and ready to be planted. You would have a full garden of flowers after all. You couldn't wait to bring them to the sun, but then feared the sun would damage them since they had been so long protected. You woke up from the dream before that problem was solved.

You have been stimulated to look for the seeds of God that were "planted" the moment you fell asleep and left Home. You did nothing to tend to them at all and thought it impossible those seedlings could have survived without water and light, but they did. This is the miracle. Each of those selves, your own inner seedlings, have "existed" in their cocoon of sleep, and now their hibernation has ended. They are hungry for the sun, ready to thrive in the Soil of Love. The children are waking up because you have found what was missing. You found the forgotten Self, the One who brings true Life to the mind of the Son. Your light had to be ignited to shine on everything tucked away inside "starter flats" in the mind. The Light of your Being is shining very brightly.

Spring is now in full bloom. The seedlings planted in My Light will grow to fulfill their glory as Children of God. Your readiness and choice to awaken has stimulated the awakening of those joined with you on the journey. It only takes one of you for the Light to surge throughout the mind. I am in charge. Do not fear that My Light is too much for the sprouts to bear. I regulate each one's growth and progression to full expansion. Leave it all to Me and live your life simply, knowing We are One, and nothing outside our Garden exists.

4

Take Your Pick

I am the Love of your Soul.
Only specialness, the desire for admiration from the world, could hide Me.

July 29, 2017

The world is cast in a spell of sleep where its inhabitants appear to have a real life, yet their true essence is hidden in disguise. There is no awakening until the realization comes that everything one sees is a mirror of either his separated self or the Love of God. You have remained covered in a blanket of sleep for lifetimes and now is the time to awaken. It is no surprise that *Beauty and the Beast* was your favorite fairy tale—it foretold your current experience of awakening to Me. Like the Beast, you have had to uncover multiple layers of costuming, which you unconsciously made to hide My Residence in you. Your specialness had to be fully recognized for you to remove the last veil covering My Essence, which you now have done. I am the Love of your Soul, and only specialness, the desire for admiration from the world, could hide Me.

The "shock" of you being forbidden to pick flowers on your condo property is what has uncovered this last layer of self-deception. You have accepted the flower taboo as a means to look at the whole world as the forbidden flower; the fruit of life as a dream. You will no longer seek the flowers/fruit of the world as a substitute for Me. I am the only Fruit, the only Flower of your Heart, and you must lose the world to gain Me. We are at the gates of Heaven with this awareness. Now you recall the opening line in *Beauty and the Beast* . . . "To pick the forbidden flowers will bring punishment forever." Yes, I led you to see the movie so you could hear that line and write this message. Those who stole a rose from the Beast's garden were turned into objects. The Beast is what the world calls Satan, the devil, the counterpart of God, but God has no counterpart because God Is. The rest is all a story; a myth no different from the story of Adam and Eve being met by the serpent who tells them to pick the fruit forbidden by God.

HS, I see that the fruit must be forbidden. It is the creation of a special self and special world separate from God. It must be forsaken in order to know unity with the One Creator and wake up from the dream. I also get that to be awake *is what matters above all else. I must be an observer of the dream from above the battleground with You at my side, knowing that everything I witness was co-created with You as a symbol of separation to wake me up. The awakened state is my reality as You. I must watch every dream character and form as a fantasy of my sleeping mind.* Yes, this is it. Dis-identify from everything you see as a story script we made to wake you up. The only flower you choose is My Love in you. It is My Love that showers you with the sweetness of Life—abundant, never-ending joy and peace, which reside within. Release all specialness to Me, and that means your little self must disintegrate into nothingness along with everything that appears to exist in this fairy tale world. Let everything go and only I remain as Real. Love is Real. God is.

5

Standing in the Middle

My "predictions" allow for an expansion of your mind.

August 3, 2017

Today you will meet your Self in a woman named Marion who is visiting you from the mainland. In the heart, you are "one soul" personified. To see your Self reflected in one who knows and loves Me is a joy, and is what you long to see in everyone you meet. Although most will be covered in veils of seeming separation, they are all waiting for the spark that will arouse their own custom course of awakening. You and Marion are on the same path so you can easily share the intimacy of your journey. You were also together during the time of Jesus. Let Me guide your visit. You will meet her this evening and go to the ukulele jam.

(Later) *Holy Spirit, Marion just canceled getting together tonight at the jam. Didn't You "predict" that we would go? Why didn't that materialize?* You have already welcomed her in the shared mind—that is what matters, but you had to count on "your plan" to hold the space of your joining. It was your ego's desire to take her to the uke jam, not Mine. If your mind had been totally given to Me you would not have had an agenda. You would have "let it flow" in My Time and in My Way. My "predictions" allow for an expansion of your mind. Accept My gifts in the Moment of Now and make no assumptions about the world. This is the opposite of visualizing and manifesting what you want in the world.

This guidance also applies to meeting Gary Renard, the author of *The Disappearance of the Universe,* who is currently giving a workshop on Maui, even though I once said you would not meet. But Now is the time for that to happen. I want you to look at all the stories the mind makes up then see how soon those thoughts change, if not each moment. Your invitation to have lunch with Gary will happen because your mind must receive that possibility. *But Holy Spirit, what if it doesn't happen?* In the dream, it has already taken place. You are "willing to not see Gary, and to see Gary." This is where I want you—right in the middle of the fulcrum. *Okay, Holy Spirit, I stand with You.*

6

Unscripted

You are only Real in the moment we share as One in the Now.

August 8, 2017

Holy Spirit, please give me clarity about "holding to a script." Jo told me she believes the script must be followed in light of a visitor coming, who she describes as difficult. She still believes her destined response is to surrender to whatever the script "assigns," and therefore thinks she does not have the option to say no. Help me understand "the script" from Your perspective for both of us.

No one is a product of the world he sees, nor of a script he has come to believe is true. There is No script and there is No world. The idea of a script is a tool to help you accept that you have "created this dream" and that I have made it with you. It is a kindergarten lesson, which you have accepted, but now must release. You do accept that your world is constructed by Me for you to learn the lessons that will bring you Home. The *Course* is a primer and you have passed it now. Let everything go, and know that I am living your life in the moment; *not* in accordance with a prewritten script. I follow no script. I have full reign now. Each moment I take you where I will with each decision you make with Me.

Jo has taken the *Course* and our books literally, believing there is a predestined script she must follow or else she will be in disharmony with God. She has not asked Me if she can say no to her guest because she believes I have prepared a specific lesson for her, and her visitor. Because she did not ask for My guidance, although she would like to tell the woman not to come, she is really saying she wants to suffer, and even blame Me for not "saving her." You, she, everyone is One with God in *this* moment. When Jo's decision maker says no to the ego scripter/script, then she can allow Me to "live her" in every moment and say no to the world without any guilt. She is not committed or obliged to answer to any call of the world. I am the only one she serves. Friends and family may plead for attention but only I am real. All must turn to Me for every aspect of their "mental/physical" life. The future unfolds with Me, and each moment you have the choice to move forward with the hand of the ego or with My Hand.

This world is just a progression of thoughts, and I am "living you" beyond this world. *We* are in the right mind taking each step, out pictured in form, because *you* have surrendered your life to Me. Release all thought and I carry you forward, further, according to My Plan for your Return. The Plan can change on a moment-by-moment basis, and indeed it does according to your readiness. I tell you, mt, that Ken Wapnick will "edit Book 1" and you accept it in that moment. Then it changes. This is My Doing, My Progression with you in the mind. You see it out pictured in what you believe is a world, but we have gone beyond that now.

When you are unsure of anything take My Hand and ask immediately for My instruction. Follow that until another moment of questioning arises and then I will answer. The answer follows no pre-prescribed pattern. It can move forward, backward, or stay in neutral. You are only Real in the moment we share as One in the Now. Release the world; release the scripts, and release the primers. They are finished. We move forward: *unencumbered* now. This is the gift of today—our "anniversary." The texts that served you to arrive at this point are now ancient history; obsolete, because you have moved beyond the limitations and attachments to form and can step into the Void with Me.

From Meera: *OMG. The magnitude of this message really hit me when I sat with the HS to find the nuggets. Each word is a pearl. No scripts! Only the NOW. Catapulted into a new paradigm. Into Eternity. This IS beyond the beyond! Freedom from the script. Moving forward from here is a challenge the HS is giving us. Takes my breath away.*

7

Old Friends

View your life experiences from a place of impersonal witnessing.

August 9, 2017

You know that each day is precisely orchestrated and that every event is perfectly timed. You, Jo, and Meera are very aware of the shared mind, having simultaneous thoughts and experiences which reflect My daily dictations. Every day's message has carried you a noticeable step further into a deeper revelation of My Mystery. You also recognize that your light is being witnessed by others. Many lives are being changed as readers are coming to hear My Voice. What is most remarkable to the three of you is the disappearance of nearly all your ego identification. You can now view your life and experiences without specialness from a place of impersonal witnessing with Me. You have no identification with or attachment to our books, but are totally dedicated to doing My Will concerning their publication. You have released the major projections of separation placed onto the significant others in your lives and have seen your one Self mirrored in many. You have allowed Me to speak through you in events, book signings, and for mt, in Toastmasters. You have no fear of tomorrow because you are assured of My Presence, Constancy, and Peace.

As you know, I have asked Gary Renard to contact you because your meeting will be as valuable for him as it will be for you. I will not give you any details because you must be a blank slate entering the conversation. I will be speaking you. It is also important for his wife Cindy and their guests to hear you speak of Me. You had not yet asked for My instruction but I am giving it to you even before you do. You know this meeting is being orchestrated by Me for My Purpose. Yes, it is about joining in a holy relationship; a holy encounter with everyone there. Welcome them all into your heart. You thought of giving Gary one of your paintings, happy to part with your "treasures," and that's a good thing. I live you both!

You and Gary are one in the mind joined with Me. Your meeting will be a Homecoming. You knew each other in the time of Jesus and had a close connection. You were not expecting Me to say that, but I have reserved it for this moment. Receive this neutrally; part of a story with no special characters, and do not dismiss your conjunction in this lifetime. It is serving My Purpose and will continue to serve you both. You are not making this up. Receive what he has to offer and be open to his understanding of Me. He will also welcome what you bring. Hold yourself in balance. This meeting will unfold as I Will. *Holy Spirit, I surrender to what is.*

8

Perfect Balance

It is a joy of deep satisfaction to be joined with those who know and live through Me.

August 11, 2017

You must identify only with the Self in your brother beneath the costume of his body and personality, and I have just shown you the contrast between a "holy encounter" and an ego confrontation. This lesson was brilliantly demonstrated by two impersonal interactions. First, you met with Gary Renard, his wife Cindy, and his guests, Gabriella and her daughter Alzena, and later you met with Zoe. During your lunch with Gary, you recognized in him the holder, the vessel, of My Kindness and My Presence. No words had to be spoken to feel the peace and love that indicated the communion between the two of you. Cindy immediately recognized you live from Me. All were held in a "holy communion of saints"—those who know Me as their Self. It is a joy of deep satisfaction to be joined with those who know and live through Me.

After your time together, you savored the lingering contentment encompassing you and decided to take a walk on a nearby road to be alone. As you left your driveway, Zoe pulled up in her car. You sensed her anger even before you mentioned that you had had lunch with Gary. When you did share that, she immediately said, "He's loony." After you replied that he and you are the same, she acknowledged that you are "sane and conscious" and that she loves you. Your encounter did not disturb your perfect balance of union with Me. Zoe represented the ego self that would disrupt your joy to prove that I do not reign supreme in you. It was a great gift to see that you are unaffected by the ego's protest to the sharing of a holy relationship. You no longer have to identify with the ego brothers you have made.

Zoe was playing her perfect part on the perfect day; nothing but a child's protest for its imagined abandonment. You had left her realm of control and her ego was feeling rejected in the dream; your dream. You smiled and did not let her comments disturb you like they used to. This was repeated while you were watching the beauty of the fading sunset from your lanai. A tourist in the condo next to you came out on his lanai swearing about the horrible view with an electrical pole and all that asphalt right in front of him. He spit over the railing and on the floor before going back inside, desecrating your "sacred land." In the past, you would have been furious, but now you are not falling for it. You saw it as just another example of how your ego is protesting the joining with Me as your *only* reality. Both Zoe and the tourist represent your ego mind that would desecrate the Kingdom of God. They were playing their roles to show you how much you have disengaged from the dream life. This marks a turning point for you. Now you are even more aware of your awakened state. The multiplicity of roles played by the thousands of dream characters cannot have any real effect on you. I am you, and we are One. Nothing else matters.

9

Influencer

The dreaming is Over
and your mind is waking up from the
nightmare of separation.

August 13, 2017

Holy Spirit, is there even a "dreamer?" Not if you never left God. The dream of being separate from God . . . life in form, bodies, a planet on which to live . . . is all a lie. It is, in fact, the opposite of God, Who only extends Love through Shining His Light. In this moment, you are "blank" and have no idea what I could even refer to in mt's life. I am living you and your world is Mine. You are not making any intentions about how your life should be, such as manifesting your ego's plans or desires. This is what it means to be fully surrendered to Me.

Last night you walked Keawakapu Beach with a friend who has lived her life in search of a deeper connection with Me. She spoke of "manifesting the beauty of the evening" that you were sharing, but you know I am the one who "manifests" everything. A dream character has no influence over the world because there is no world. Period. Your friend did not make the beautiful sunset on the beach nor arrange your time to be together. When you are speaking with others, you must be clear that I am the only "force" alive in you and in them. It appears to be a subtle point, but is the heart of the next step in the awakening process. *How should I respond when friends speak of manifestation?* Allow them to state their thoughts, and if they ask, let them know that you are allowing Me to live you. They will feel it, and when they are ready, they will come to Me. You "signal" that there is further for them to go.

All are One with God. The dreaming is Over and your mind is waking up from the nightmare of separation. I show the Way to everyone's full awakening. See only your Self everywhere you go; it is the Holy Face of God you encounter. God Is. Nothing exists outside of Him, so what the separated mind projects as "real" is nothing other than a mirage. You must realize that "you and this universe and beyond" is just what you imagine came from God the Creator. God creates no form. This idea is very confusing to a mind not yet aware that *it is God.* These are some of the last distinctions to be made by an "awakening dreamer."

10

A Play of Light and Dark

You may not see My Brilliance but you can feel My Presence within.

August 20, 2017

I am with you and you do not "disappointment Me" when you miss seeing the very last sliver of the rising moon. The loss of being there at "just the right time" comes from your ego that has not magically determined the perfect moment to look, or have the patience to wait for it to rise. This is the synopsis of your ego life. It wants what it wants when it wants it. If its desire is not fully met, it is unhappy and severely chastises you. As an ego character you feel you are worthless because you can't make anything "right." The ego is always thwarted; its "best" intentions never fully met. This is what it means to live from the ego's will. Although you desire to live from My Will alone, the ego still pops up with its agenda.

Now you smile as you realize that tomorrow thousands of people will be traveling to see the new moon cover the sun, leaving their world in darkness. Only a small ring of the sun's corona will be visible. And you are upset because you didn't see a sliver of moonlight? These two images coincide on the day before the eclipse. This event is nothing but a play of light and dark; the experience of duality in one fell swoop. The light of the moon was in its last phase this morning, and the light of the sun will soon be obliterated—the false disappearance of the Light of God. You already sense the "dream of life on earth" as the shadow that will pass over the planet. You all live in a shadow of separation from God, your Source, the Light of your Life. You may not see My Brilliance but you can feel My Presence within. And no, you cannot imagine what it will be like to know Me, your Self, as the Light of the Universe.

The sun and moon repeat their phases and you count on their permanence, but an eclipse can shake up the split mind by showing that its false light can be "turned off" in a second. This would be the ending of the dream world. This is what the ego fears above all else that the Light of the Son, the True Light, will return. It is this thought that will be stimulated in the unconscious mind of all who are present, or who watch through the media. The sun and the moon, symbols of My Light and Constancy, will be "reorganized" in the mind of man, allowing Me a moment of intervention to remind humanity of Me, of My Resurrection. You will read accounts of this after the event, and I want you to have this foretelling before it happens. All those participating will be touched. You have essentially "left" the world and need not be there to experience it first hand, but you will experience the vibration of those awakening in the mind you share. Watch all the sun gazers and know the True Sun is shining within each one. The eclipse can be a stimulus to seek beyond "sun and moon" to find the Source of True Light. I do Light the Way.

11

Not Even a Speck

You say I live within you, but that is false. I Am you.

August 24, 2017

You are with Me; a Part of Me. We are "inseparable Beingness." Your Essence is My Essence. You say I live within you, but that is false. I Am you. I am what is Real and I am not form. Nothing of mt contains Me. She is just a projected image; a mere thought. Her brain is not what thinks or imagines. Last night you watched the documentary *The Farthest—Voyager in Space* about the Voyager 1 spacecraft, which looked back from interstellar space to take a picture of your solar system after leaving it. Earth was noticed as a speck of dust shining in the far background. You are not even a speck of dust. I am your mind and you are a nano-thought of separation amidst the Cosmos of God's Mind.

None of the images of galaxies beyond galaxies are real outside the mind that seeks and projects them. You were pleased to hear that Voyager had entered interstellar space in August of 2012, the same month you also left the confines of identification with your limited mt mind. It was then you heard My Voice, which took you into the reality of your Self beyond time and space. Your full awakening is on track. You will reach your destination, just as will the golden record onboard Voyager 1 before it finally disappears.

The Voyager program reminded you of a book you read in the 70s, *Bringers of the Dawn,* "channeled" by beings from the Pleiades. They are no more real than the speck of mt; thoughts of a separated mind holding on to the idea of life on a distant planet.

There are no worlds, no solar systems, no interstellar space. They are just symbols made up to represent the Vastness of the Mind of God which is your inheritance. The Sonship is a microcosm of God; the expansion, extension of "the universe." Let go of the earth and all its contents. We are almost Home.

12

The Blessing of Betrayal

Everyone who seems to betray you has been instrumental in bringing you back to Me.

September 1, 2017

You are with Me now and forever. Everything and everyone, the sky and the earth, is Me embracing you. This morning you awoke with a dream that gave just that message.

Dream: *It was late in the afternoon when Tom decided we would drive along the coast to visit a friend of his at her library. The trip would take hours and I wanted to call ahead to ensure she'd be there, although I was aware the Holy Spirit would be in charge. Before we knew it, we arrived at the library and it was still open. There were papers on the floor and indications that Tom's friend was there. He called to her and soon a number of people appeared. Then I found myself sitting in the lap of a very large Santa Claus figure with a Southern accent. I was in total comfort as he expressed his impersonal love for me. I didn't need to know his true identity, somehow sensing he had known me forever. I knew the comfort of being in his lap and that the Holy Spirit had arranged this conjunction. When I woke up, I did wonder who the man was because he was so familiar. It came to me that he was Tom's father who had always loved me as a daughter-in-law until one day, after I had given him a foot massage, he exclaimed, "You don't know how to love people. You can only love animals." It was a shock to all present, and I assumed that it was his own ego projection, but it caused a rift in our relationship. This morning's dream brought peace and resolution.*

You do know your "dream Santa" was Me, and that I always hold you in My Love. Everything in your world is a reflection of that Love. I never leave you comfortless when you think of Me and am always showering you with My blessings. The night dream was meant to resolve the yet unsettled rift that took place between you and your father-in-law. You experienced his love, but you know he represented Me in the world of time. Both Tom and his father loved you dearly. You all are/were under My Love and protection. Everyone who has ever seemed to "betray you" was instrumental in bringing you back to Me. Through their seeming rejections they set you free to move forward and find Me. I use them all to teach you this lesson in the classroom of life. Behind the experiences of discord, My Love still comes through and is carrying you to your destiny as One with God. The misperceptions of a separated world have been lifted so now you see with My Vision a world of Love.

Yesterday, *OWG Book 3* arrived at Jo's home. It is a big book, as she said. It is also an important manifesto of My Love for humanity and will be read widely. I timed the appearance of our new book with the arrival of Jo's nemesis; a visit she had believed would cause her to suffer. But Jo's fears evaporated when she saw that her ego imaginings were false. By giving herself and her life totally to Me, she has found supreme peace. The ego's expressions of its fear of love will always vanish in the Arms of My Embrace. Every visitor, in day or night dreaming, is an instrument of My Love, which turns the tables on fear and hatred and brings resolution to everything believed to be a problem. There are no problems so I am the only Solution. We are One with God and we join together now in a Happy Dream.

13

All the Same

To be an individual is to be special;
in other words, to be apart from the Wholeness of God Is.

September 18, 2017

You are working with the concept of specialness, seeing it was the idea of specialness that "created" the world, bodies, and the dream itself. Without it, no individuality could ever exist. To be an individual is to be special; in other words, to be apart from the Wholeness of God Is. The ego self, the essence of specialness, came from a belief that something outside of God could exist; could be created. But outside of the dream, there is only Unity. God is One. In God there is no other. The Son is God's Extension. There is no differentiation in True Sonship. The "sonship" of humanity is just a conglomeration of individual selves, loosely co-existing in various degrees of separation, believing they are real.

This morning you came to realize there can be No "elevated" beings in a dream. A dream is a dream and has no value. It is meaningless and composed of nothing but a thought passing through a mind asleep. To be elevated in any respect negates the statement from *ACIM* that there is No hierarchy of illusions. You also had the clarity that the gurus, who you have all but revered, are just dream characters; projection screens for one's desire to be above God, superior to God. Yes, that is how the guru is perceived by his devotee. The guru is a substitute for the devotee's desire to achieve "individual" Godhood, revered by all, to the exclusion of the One God. And yes, that is what happens in every ashram, where the thousands chant to their guru as "Lord of the Universe."

You have done that hundreds of times yourself as mt seeking spiritual elevation.

Now that the "heights" are cut down to size, and the "size" is down to nothing, there are no heights to scale, no ladders of transformation and consciousness to climb. You are all the One Son, made from the same clay, returning to ashes after the ego is burned away. This is a big realization and it has taken many years, let alone lifetimes, to approach the knowing that to be One with God, the individual must be nothing—nothing but a passing cloud in a sky of separation. We are One with God and all beings are included in that Oneness. You smile, knowing there is no hierarchy of illusion among your friends the crabs. They all display "crabness" even though some are larger, stronger, and can squirt farther than the others. There is only "a thought of crab" which includes them all. When gathered together they could hardly be differentiated. They are one. When man is looked upon outside of the solar system, he does not exist at all, no matter how many vigintillion beings there appear to be. He is nothing but a tiny mad idea of specialness. Let it go, knowing you are not "special" to Me because We are Everything; One and the Same.

14

Tear Up the List

This world cannot contain you, sustain you, or define you.

September 27, 2017

In this morning's dream you were in a room, not clearly delineated, with a woman who was more of an apparition than a solid body. She was quite distressed and asked you to return the "list of attributes" you had taken from her. You frantically searched for the list, which you could envision on a yellow lined piece of paper, but no pile of papers contained it. You even blindly pushed a stack of sheets into a knick-knack shelf breaking its unseen objects in your attempt to locate it.

This dream holds an important lesson and observation. I asked you to sit with Me on the lava rocks to consider it. You realized that the attributes mentioned in the dream were only those of an ego self in a made-up world. It then occurred to you, today being your father's birthday, that he was not your maker or creator, but was a projection of Me, the Holy Spirit, Who brought you into this world to learn just this lesson—you are not your body, or its characteristics, and you do not come from the world of form. Your birth father was only a symbol; a substitute for your Father in Heaven, but he held you throughout your life in his love. That was My Love, and your father played his part perfectly. You grew up believing he was real and felt total trust of his love for you. That never faltered. It was his modeling of the constancy of that love which allowed you to Trust that My Love for you is Constant.

You have released the world and are incorporating that realization into the deepest recesses of your being. There is nothing here for you to hold onto, which you also saw in the night dream. This world cannot contain you, sustain you, or define you. You have gone "beyond it" in your mind. Even living in a place called "paradise" does not bring a desire to return to this earth. You are done with form, and the attributes of your body and world. I made them with you as pointers in your life script to bring you to this realization. Hold fast to Me. We are One and you will continue living out your dream days "in the world but not of it" until My purpose for you is done. Continue to write and publish the words I give you. Heaven's doors are now opening.

15

The Certainty Principle

The world is nothing but a calculation of the mind.

October 2, 2017

I have given you the "equation for life" and it is this: *Life = God. God Is.* This was shown to you in a dream right before you woke up where you were standing beside two young female physicists. They were both holding sheets of white paper containing simple arithmetic of addition and subtraction. As they were speaking about the math problems, you were imagining the blackboard equations of Einstein or Hawking in all their complexity. Finally, you asked the women in all seriousness, "*What do your equations really tell?*" Their answer was—"the solution is a probability." Tremendous relief and freedom filled your being and that surprised you. It was as if the problem of the universe was solved. So simply put! The one solution of all the world's greatest conundrums could only be a probability; therefore, no problem could really be true. Then you spoke to the women as one, their heads against a background of sky. You asked if they *really trusted* that they were in the Hands of God, would they still need equations? You then proclaimed, "The universe and all math is nothing if it isn't the Certainty of God." In that very moment, you knew My Certainty and you wiped out the world. Nothing existed but Me/God. *That* was a moment of Truth. The world disappeared. Every "other" was gone. Only you and I remained as One. *That* is Freedom.

HS, why did I have that dream today? I wanted to emphasize that the world is nothing but a calculation of the mind and the solution to everything is Me, God. In Me, everything is Solved; everything is Certain. Place this concept solidly in your mind because it is All you need to live the rest of your life on earth. The earth is a probability, a thought of a separated mind that asked what it would be like to live apart from God. The answer from that mind was a probability suggesting a wondrous life but without examples of the possible outcomes, so you were willing to take your chances.

Now you trust nothing and no one but Me, accepting only My Solution as true for you. We are going past the world, leaving it all behind. I am the Only Certainty that Is. This is the point of our books—to carry this Thought, which I am transmitting through you, and through all those awakening from this "probability" you have called life. It is just a dream and nothing more—just figment after figment of possibilities for manifestations that seem to become real in a world that is only a puff of wind.

Hold fast to Me as you fly above the clouds of space and time, which you will experience in a few days with your friend Pat on a parasail over the ocean. It is to be a symbol of the Return Home—soon to be your reality. Enjoy the Ride. I am with you in every particle of the experience: the boat, the chair, the ropes, the ocean below, the sky above. Every quantum of Life is Mine. Leave everything to Me. I am your Certainty. I am God. And we are One.

16

There IS a Better Way

There is a purpose for everything, which I use for you to experience the imagined separation from Me.

October 15, 2017

From Meera: *A dear high school friend Arlene, who has worked closely with Holocaust survivors, became particularly close with a woman named Frieda and told me about her autobiography. When I shared with Arlene that I hear the Still Small Voice of the Holy Spirit, she mentioned that Frieda received what she called "spontaneous writing" that was directive and very meaningful to her. I was led to connect with Frieda. We chatted a couple of times and exchanged a few emails. I then asked the Holy Spirit about the significance of our connection. He said:* I have put Frieda's autobiography in your hands for you to see what I spared you from. Frieda is a reflection of your "struggle and soul." You are One. Her path was to physically plod through the most heinous atrocities imaginable and to come out with a strong spirit, knowing I "choreographed" it all. There is no way the human mind can comprehend the depth of hatred/evil that operates in the dream. Frieda experienced it and was at the brink of death when her concentration camp was liberated in April of 1945. You were two months old at the time.

I have shown you, Meera, two previous incarnations . . . one at the gas chambers at age ten, when parting from your mother, who said, "Someday you will grow up where it is safe to be a Jew." I then brought you right back as an infant where your mother smothered you on a cattle car heading to the gas chamber to prevent your demise at the hands of the Nazis. You have carried with you the horror that permeated those lifetimes; the grief, the sadness, and guilt that must finally be released. You did nothing wrong. You were a "victim" of the darkest hours of the ego mind as fear and hate overrode love and peace, out pictured as a projection of attack, attack, attack in Nazi Germany and other countries. Ever since, you have retreated, hiding behind a false persona that hobbled through a life wrapped in guilt, yet always sensing there was a better way.

This week, when you did your volunteer hospital rounds, you first visited a ninety-two-year-old Holocaust survivor who said her husband and son were, and are, "evil devils" and that the people who expired in the gas chambers were luckier than she who had lived a life of hell. When you asked Me for help in what to say to her you heard nothing. There was nothing to say. You were just to witness the projection of hatred and fear carried forward. Only then did I have you say that she must forgive her son. Next you visited with another Holocaust survivor, also in her nineties, who was in total gratitude to be so well taken care of. She shared how her three children are loving and supportive and you witnessed the gentle kindness of her phone conversation with her son. These two responses perfectly contrast the split mind of fear and separation versus Love, Peace, and Unity. There is a purpose for everything, which I use for you to experience the imagined separation from Me because separation exists only in the mind. Know that you are unraveling the end of the mind's contamination, removing the last of the darkness so you can return Home unencumbered by the past. I now have your cousin telling you from beyond the beyond: "None of it matters." NONE of this world is real.

17

What Are You Arranging?

Form is forgotten, but the Content—My Presence—
is what touches.

October 18, 2017

You live in a world of images and assumptions, assuming what you see is true. Your ego self wants everything to materialize right before your eyes as you imagine it. This early morning, you hoped to see the last hint of the moon but it never appeared. Then you wanted to hear the final stanzas of a Mozart symphony but our writing took precedence. In this world of form, things will never happen the way your ego mind desires it to be, which you experienced last night at Toastmasters when you gave a demonstration of Ikebana flower arranging. But now you can't even recall what you said, let alone why the audience would say they loved it. It doesn't matter what you say. It is My Presence in you that makes a speech or anything worthwhile. As you spoke, the members felt Me, My Light, shining in you. Form is always forgotten but the Content—My Presence of Comfort and Inclusion—is what touches; what remains. This you do not yet understand. Mt is still caught up in the details of her life and what she presents to the world. Details will all slip away, just as the "setting" of the moon represents its obliteration. The world does not exist. Only My Ever-Present Light is Real.

(Later) *Holy Spirit, I have been thinking about all the hours mt had put into the collection of branches and flowers to make the arrangements for the Toastmaster's speech, but in the end it all seemed worthless. A big poster blocked the view while I spoke, and many flowers were not even used. Yes, I did enjoy the process but it could be seen as a distraction. What do You say?* Only see the elements of the world in your Ikebana container symbolically . . . placed the way you wanted yet appearing helter-skelter. In the end, the "arrangement" is not as lovely as you had hoped. No one showed lasting interest in what you even did. This is the way of "life in the world" in one mini-lesson.

One's "work" is just a token of loyalty to the establishment, whatever it may be. What you do or don't do in the world makes no difference. You are all waiting to die. I say die to the body and die to the ego. Flowers will wither away just as will you. It doesn't matter that they lived and then died. That sounds harsh but it is the truth. You dance your dance and it is forgotten the very next moment. Remember that none of what I say means anything to your ego mind. It calls you over and over to believe it is real and to think that your presence on this earth is necessary. It is not your mt presence that changes anything. It is My Presence in you that reaches out to all your selves and brings kinship at the deepest level to the Sonship. Wake up from this dream and I Am There.

18

Lit

Every speck of darkness will be overtaken by Me.

October 19, 2017

You have "seen Me." Yes, I gave you a visual in your mind—a "white light" that appeared behind closed eyes while you were outside your front door waiting for Venus to rise. You could not imagine how that pure white light could have formed, thinking somehow it had been stimulated by the dull incandescent lamps scattered around your property. No, it was not the outer world that produced that light. It was I.

My Light outshines and obliterates all the world's light. It is more powerful than that of all the stars and galaxies. You would describe what you "saw" as a merging of two amorphous spheres of light coalesced into one circle. And yes, a tiny black hole, a speck, the size of the planet Venus as seen from Earth, appeared to be in the center. You had a moment of concern but you know that every speck of darkness will be overtaken by Me. You look at a picture of your self as it appears in the world of dreams, but I see your Light; your reality within. Now you have seen Its image. Your ego mind told you that something must be wrong with you to have that vision of Light. Nothing is wrong. The black speck in the middle is a symbol of the ego that would like to be at the center of your world, but you see its dimming power and that it can never take over My Light. The questioning part of your mind can't believe what I tell you or even show you is real. Yes, your trust is increasing daily, but a dot of doubt remains. That too will go before you awaken.

You are right, HS, because I think I'm making up this whole message. I want it all to be true. I want to be the Light. Mt still identifies with the tiny black dot yet Venus jumped up over the mountain and its light would just fill that dark spot. Do I project my light, Your Light, out into the world instead of accepting it as my Reality? I want Total Light with no dark spots, Holy Spirit. Bring me to Wholeness. Just bring the Light back into your mind as your Christ Self.

Last night you saw a report of the discovery of a collision of two neutron stars that altered the fabric of space. Everything you see in the world is a picture of what is happening in your mind. As the world collapses, just as the collapse of a star, you enter the place of nothingness. Some would call it a black hole, but it symbolizes the disappearance of the universe and the coming Home to the Light of God as all that is. You are not making this up as your ego would want you to believe. I am with you and I carry you the next step, every step of the way Home, faster than the speed of light.

19

The Rub

Abandon the self-taught edict that you were "born to suffer" and that only suffering would bring you Home.

October 25, 2017

You watch the rain and feel a moment of guilt for not suffering, like those now dealing with the area floods. The belief that to suffer more than others would make someone "more deserving" of Heaven's riches feels like the same belief that you once needed to be the best, the "goodest" girl in the world because the ones who either endure the most, or who are morally the highest, would win the prize. Mankind believes that each one is "doomed" to suffer; a belief that accompanies each being as they enter the world of form with their birth. You recall how your mother had suffered immensely and that you could not "hold" her suffering. How could you begin to hold the suffering of Jesus on the cross? Yet in this moment, you see that all mankind has been subjected to the fear of being tortured and killed in heinous ways. Even Jesus was not special in the form of persecution he underwent. And *he* was a good man; the "best man in the world," yet appeared to suffer a tortuous demise. Yes, there is the rub. And that is what makes the whole story on earth so confusing and fearful.

If you are the best, the goodest person in the world, must you end your life in the greatest suffering to deserve the return to Heaven? No, that does not make sense. Deep inside, you always knew you'd never be good enough, but you still tried. You always thought you *feared* the discomfort that would gain you the reward of eternal life, but you actually *desired* it. There was no way to win. Now that you know Me, you can see the silliness and falseness of the belief in separation and pain. It stymies you from living a life of joy. The concept of joy is still just a notion because you have never known True Joy. To know Joy would mean that you had abandoned the self-taught edict that you were "born to suffer" and that only suffering would bring you Home.

In this moment, you see that you never really thought of Heaven in terms of "Home." Only since you have known Me and read the *Course* have you realized that I am synonymous with Home. Heaven was just an amorphous concept of being saved from hell. You never conceived of it as a return to Love or to your Father in a way that would bring you the Joy of Union. That was not imaginable because you had not yet developed a "personal relationship" with Me. The idea of the Return now can bring an expectation of joy because it means joining with Me in the love that you already feel has expanded exponentially. This is important for all to look at. You all have the same belief in one form or another that you are not worthy of God's Love and do not deserve Heaven. That belief is the basis of the original separation and the beginning of time. We are eradicating that idea now from the one mind.

You are all in Heaven, now. Heaven is Home as One with God. We live in the Mind of God, not in a projected distant world of form that is a mirage of hell. Hell cannot exist because you live in God. There is no heaven or hell outside of you. You each made your own hell with the belief you must suffer in order to be worthy of God and have punished yourself with this idea from the very beginning. Enough! Terminate that idea now and forever. You are "born" into the Hands of God, then spend your "life" dreaming of finding your way back home, only to learn you have been cradled in His Love for all Eternity. Awaken to the awareness that you were never born and will never die. You have always been held in the Arms of Love, the Love of God, which you are. We are the Kingdom of God and you *are* Home.

20

Memory of the Cross

We are One and there is nothing for which to be guilty.

November 15, 2017

Holy Spirit, thank You for this beautiful morning and for the gift of being able to scribe Your words. Listening to Cindy Renard's song about the crucifixion, I had an image in my mind of Jesus drooped over on the cross. Was that a "real" memory? Yes, you did see Me as Jesus on the cross. I gave you that image today to bring you closer yet to the reality of our communion, and also for you to look more deeply at the origin of your guilt in association with Jesus. This is why you have been drawn to Gary Renard's books and to Cindy's music. They were there too. *But I always thought I kept my distance from Jesus and was angry with him.* Internally, you were compelled to know him more deeply, but you also had to see for yourself that the crucifixion took place. When he slumped over in death, you were relieved and secretly happy his life had ended. To see him leave the earth gave you relief from your feelings of separation during his lifetime . . . you wanted to be free of the secret guilt over your anger at him; free of the need to make amends. Because you did not feel included, you assumed that I, as Jesus, neglected you.

This morning you begged Me to help you remain invisible as mt and "be" only Me, the Holy Spirit. This is where you have come on the journey to see Me, Jesus, your Self, as One and the Same. The guilt you had about the desire to see Jesus "out of your life" can now vanish. What happened "at the cross" was the duplication for you of leaving Heaven in the original separation, which was overwhelming and deeply repressed. Yet your heart did recognize Me in Jesus and held the memory of what you had left behind. Can you "witness the death" of your made-up character mt? Now is the time of our Reunion and your recognition of the story that has held you back from Me for lifetimes. We are One and there is nothing for which to be guilty. You were meant to scribe these books and they had to come from one who was born with unresolved guilt. Your story has to be fully expressed and exposed to you and the readers. All have a similar story hidden deep in the recesses of their mind. Today you come Home.

But HS, I don't feel any different, no great liberation or joy, and I really can't grok the reality of what You tell me about being at the crucifixion. I do get that to be a scribe for Your books, I had to have a real knowing of You deep in my soul. That would have been the driving force to devote myself to this journey. Yes, that is what drives you. Deep in your mind you knew Me as your reality and that is why you love Cindy Renard's song describing her connection with Jesus, including her pain and guilt at his death. You are one with her in your connection to Me. You are to complete the work I have given you in this life to bring My Teachings, the Teachings of Jesus, to the world. The lesson is simple—you are all One with God. You now recall from *ACIM*: *"The holiest of all the spots on earth is where an ancient hatred has become a present love. . . . Where stood a cross, now stands the risen Christ, and ancient scars are healed within His sight"* (T.26.IX.6;8).

21

Blowing in the Wind

There is nothing to complete to make you whole in a dream.

December 5, 2017

You are One with Me and this you are getting. This became even clearer with your night dream of lying on a bed in a house you believed was yours, while it was being carried forward by a silent, invisible wind. You knew the house would eventually have to land or crash and there was nothing you could do. You thought of Dorothy in *The Wizard of Oz* and you continuously called on Me, yet having no fear. Then you woke up. This is the way it will be. This is all there is to the end of the world—no different from falling into the void. You are carried and held in an unseen Energy that completes itself. Yes, that is a lovely thought: *It completes Itself.* You come to completion by waking up.

There is nothing to complete to make you whole in a dream. You are already Whole, One with God. Nothing else. The completion is in the awakening. Rest assured I have every detail of your life handled. I am the Energy of Life that carries you Home, not unlike the invisible dream wind. We together are the Power that "forms the universe." You will fully awaken and will know that Power as your Self. This is why you have seen Dorothy on the movie screen, and more recently, a "Dorothy character" in *Chitty Chitty Bang Bang,* who flies home in a magic car. You have the faith of a child now; you simply trust Me and know I will bring you Home. You are the red shoes and the magic car and

Homeward we go. Fear is gone when your life is given to Me. Nothing else is needed.

Holy Spirit, am I where You want me to be? Yes, you are not identified with the dream—no more goals, no more past or future, and no more guilt. *I accept this Holy Spirit . . . not with feelings, just acceptance. Nothing different . . . a realization that makes the whole dream story meaningless, and of course the story seems to be playing out so mt still has an ego and her tasks. I am just not identified with her as my Reality. This state feels so inconsequential. I am that I am and I accept that. There are no bells and whistles. The dream offers nothing. It is Done, it is Over, it is an illusion. The* I AM *Knows Itself as the Christ. I am just accepting What Is. HS, is there more I should know?* You are in the Peace of God. Know that this is the state of awakening from the dream life. Know yourself as Me. There is nothing else to know; nowhere else to go. Let the wind blow. We are beyond all dreaming.

22

The Only Salvation

To "save the world" means to leave the world and return to the memory of God.

December 10, 2017

You have looked at the dream with Me. You saw its nothingness. Nothing about it is sacred. The dream is the Anti-Christ exposed, the belief that God does not exist and that man rules the universe. God was wiped out of the mind the moment the separation took place with the tiny mad idea that you could be independent of Him. The dream world is the opposite of God and His Kingdom. It would be Its replacement, Its substitute. Man seats himself on a throne as the god of his world. You see this clearly depicted when you turn on the media. The news is focused on threats and attacks, war and winning, which compose life on this planet. It is the essence of duality, which will forever negate itself because good and bad are interchangeable given the time and circumstances. You killed whales in your last lifetime and this time you treasure them. The teeter totter world will never balance itself out and conflict will reign until man wakes up to say, "there must be a better way."

You wonder about acts of kindness and goodness and the efforts to save the oceans, the trees, and the animals while you watch fires consuming the forests, and chemicals destroying life on land and sea. Nothing here is safe. Everything is exposed to torture and death because everything here is an instrument of torture and death. No one is exempt because there is only One Son of God. As a conglomeration of the many selves in the split mind, the world employs a joint action to destroy the Kingdom of God before God destroys His Son. Look at the conglomerate now. Only One Son made the choice to leave Heaven. The world you see is his/your projection of the horror of that thought of separation. How does it all end? Wake up! Waking up is the only salvation. It is not about saving the earth or humankind; salvation is about knowing it is all a bad dream; a never-ending nightmare. The dream itself cannot be saved because a dream is nothing. To "save the world" means to leave the world and return to the memory of God.

It's like your night dream where you were in a white-walled, high-ceilinged, pristine bathroom where someone had painted large swatches of Eros Pink paint all over the walls. You then decided to make huge splashes of the bright pink as well. Later you were speaking to some women who were gathered for a spiritual conference and wanted them to know how you had expressed your feelings on the wall of the bathroom, adding that you would be wiping them off. It seemed perfectly logical to be so forthright, but later you feared your "expression" would not be understood. In the next scene a woman started to tell you about an investigation. You then believed you would be imprisoned for what you had done to the walls, even though you had no feelings of wrong doing or maliciousness when you expressed yourself in such a way. You knew that everything "painted" could be erased. You were transparent in describing your actions and had no fear or guilt until everyone disappeared and you were left "accountable."

Yes, only One makes up the dream and only One is accountable. In the beginning of time, you innocently proclaimed your desire for independence out of the sight and range of God, which led to a world that would imprison you forever. Guilt entered in and there was no way to explain your "mistake "—an innocent attempt at "self-expression." Now we look on that innocence, which includes this whole insane world. I am the only route out, and I will obliterate the thought of separation from your mind. The dream will end and you will return to the Kingdom you never left.

23

Sands of Time

My Presence can never leave you because It is you.

January 8, 2018

I am One with you. *HS, that is the opposite of what You usually say. Why?* You are One with Me and We are the Same. There is nothing separate from the I AM, the One God, the One Son. Get over all sense of separateness. You have identified with the body for eons, which was really just an instant. You do see the dream as a dream, and it *is* over. Yesterday that became even more clear as you saw what appeared to be "your" sand sculptured tomb with the name "Lewis" at the entrance, beneath ground level. It was no coincidence that you looked at the resting place of your last lifetime, there in the sand. You will not *die* in this lifetime because mt will have disappeared before her death, designated only in a dream, and there will be no need for commemoration of mt's body. She does not exist.

HS, this is a strange way of saying that I die before I die. Yes, and I am shaking you up to look with My Vision at what you have only imagined. We buried Lewis, you, last night. *Why not "Marjorie" on the tomb?* Because you identify with Lewis in the mind and that is where all this is happening. Lewis was very much alive to you as you read about the sea captain John Franklin sailing to the North Pole. He sailed to his death. The past is dead. Mt is gone. I live you now and I want "you," the part of your mind that tries to maintain the feeling of separateness, to fully wake up. *Help me, HS. I talk to You in the mind and I hear Your words. They are different from mt's speech. How can I feel our unity?* Each breath brings you closer to our Unity, which only means your realization of our ever-present Union. As you come closer to Me, you recede from the world. Yesterday, in the midst of a hula class, you called on Me over and over. You did not want the actions of the many dancers to hinder your concentration on the Hawaiian song—*Pua Olena,* the turmeric flower; a song dedicated to My Love and Beauty as "the awakening of sleeping flowers" in My Garden.

Last night you watched a video of Immaculée Ilibagiza. She spoke of her book *Left to Tell,* which describes her experience of being hidden in a bathroom for three months with eight other women to protect them from death in the Rwandan genocide. She is you. Her story is yours. She found Me through a constant focus on My Presence and you have done the same. My Presence can never leave you because It is you. I AM *you,* but you must stay alert to Me as your only Reality. Nothing of the world can really interfere with Me. I am not of this world. I am always in your mind. Stay conscious of Me. When you call, I answer.

Now you understand. The fear of death was the "stimulus" for Immaculée to continuously call on Me. I was her only salvation and escape from the dream of death and destruction. She demonstrates My Salvation, and her book has sold millions of copies. Our books take the reader the next step in showing that all can wake up from this insane world. You saw your tomb in the sand. Now let the world go. Know that you are Me and that we Are One with God. We have come a long way and still have a ways to go. I bring you Home in tiny incremental steps, but you are really Home this moment.

24

No More Hiding

This is the time for choice.
Either you choose Life in Me or death.

January 14, 2018

We are One. You just saw the last sliver of moon, and beneath it the planets Saturn and Mercury; the Solar System is revealed as the ego thought system is diminished. We are coming to the essentials now. Last night you dreamed of being in your former home, but the empty ground floor was almost the size of a tennis court. The stone walls had been painted and the blue counter-tops were badly scratched. You wondered how you could have lived there and had no sense that you still did. The dream house denotes the disappearance of your world. The rising and setting of the planets are your grounding now. They bring you deep satisfaction. Yes, that is strange, because you want to let the world go to come to Me alone. Yesterday you had another taste of the end of your life on earth. Include your notes here:

I got to the farmer's market early and the normally full lot was almost empty. The sale of food starts exactly at 8:30, but the last of the people were in line and the rest had already gone. It felt surreal and even more so when someone explained that everyone had gotten a cell phone message to "take cover" because of an impending missile attack. It was a hoax, but the surreal feeling hung over the morning. I had no *fear but fear was in the air. As I walked the beach, it was clear to me that I was ready to die. Nothing would hold me to this earth. I envisioned the OWG books in the void of space representing the Mind of God. I have done my work, and will remain until my "time" is up.*

Yes, you were shocked that the parking lot for the market was almost empty when you arrived, but you had not yet heard the government alert twenty minutes earlier that "a missile is heading for Hawaii—take immediate cover—this is not a drill." The alert remained active for thirty-eight minutes and left the state in a panic. People were running for cover or joining with their loved ones for a last goodbye. This was a taste of the end of life and a wakeup call for the planet. Visitors from all over the world were affected and will report that experience as the most significant of their vacation to Maui.

The whole world was once again reminded of the vulnerability of the human species. There is nowhere to hide anymore. No one is exempt. It is all or nothing. Wake up from the dream or die in a nuclear holocaust. The bottom line is Life in Me or death. Love or fear. The state of Hawaii was taken over by fear and you could feel it in the air all day. You had no fear but the vibration was palpable. The world of time and battles is a fantasy that can evaporate in the same moment as a nuclear blast. *Holy Spirit, did You plan the false alarm for today?* Yes, it is the outward picture of your inner condition—the disappearance of the universe. *I have no regrets and no desires. I'm ready to sink into the void. I know You and there is no fear.* Yes, you are done; nothing holds you to this earth; nothing more to see or do, and nowhere to go. The books have served their purpose and will continue in the mind. You will be here a while longer but you are not attached. You have chosen Me, your Self, our Unity with God, and can let the world slip away.

25

Last Symbol of Power

You will never be satisfied in the world because it is not your Home.

January 24, 2018

You have seen the end of time. It is the detachment from the earthly symbol of power: the penis. You dreamed of being with Tom in a bed; the same spot where you abandoned your pet hamster after he bit you in your childhood home, placing it in a cage outside under a pine tree. In your dream with Tom, neither of you were in bodies, but his detached, engorged penis was lying on a sheet in the deeply shadowed space. You had no emotional attachment or desire for physical union but wanted to give Tom some pleasure by rubbing the penis. No climax was reached. You are reluctant to place this in the book, but it is important to show how the dream of your life ends. You are touching the last symbol, the penis, which in Freudian interpretation is the symbol of the snake. It is the tool that lures the selves to return for endless lifetimes to have their dreams materialize; their unmet desires fulfilled. And yes, it is the instrument that inseminates to make the dream real with generation after generation of more and more selves. As you envision the detached penis, it reminds you of the pointer sticks used by teachers in your classrooms, and the lingam stone statues in Hawaii and India, symbols for the gods. Your dream of life with Tom was a pointer for your return Home.

Now that you have released the earth you can easily look at the last remnants. You will not go home again to your parents' house or to the home you left in Denver. There is no home on this earth. Nothing on earth can contain the Light and Power of God. You must be together as One with Me in the place of Light, outside the black night of nothingness. No satisfaction can be gained by lifeless things. I am the only Life there is. You will never be satisfied in this or any world. Today is Tom's birthday and you will call him, although there is nothing to be said. The communion is blocked, cut off, just as the penis in the dream. You are done with longing for your Adam—your attachment to life separate from God. You must see this played out in symbols in order to understand what I am saying. Your night dream symbolizes the detachment of all lifetimes and there is no reason to return to more dreaming. You think of your last visit to Denver, seeing how a huge hailstorm had destroyed Tom's yard. It was a sign of the end of time. You are through with the earth. Let it go. It/Tom cannot be regained.

Tom was your substitute for God. Now you look with Me, your God Self, at what you made up. It has no attraction. It is shadow. It doesn't matter. Leave it all behind. You are the hamster without a home, rejected by the world, but really you have chosen to reject the world and all its contents. You are leaving this realm of shadow and sadness, returning to your real Home with Me. You made your last effort to satisfy the world, to please the other in the dream with Tom, but you no longer want or need the other. It was just a projection of your "lost connection" with Me. There is nothing more the dream can give. Let it go.

HS, I am filled with gratitude for the unfolding of the dream and for Tom's commitment to his resistance and vow Not to communicate; not to respond to my desire for deep communion. It had to be this way to come to You. It is what the Vedic Astrologer told me many years ago, that I needed a remote Saturnian husband so I would find my Self. It has happened and I am grateful to Tom for his commitment to his vows. I have been faithful to my vow to return to You. The penis could not be inserted and I have been forever grateful that I was barren, and leave no attachments to this life in form. Thank You, HS, for bringing me back to

You as my One and Only Love. Do You have any more to say? No, you have said it all. You have incorporated the knowing of Me as your Self. We are One; One Voice.

(Later) *I feel so full and happy that Tom didn't resist when I called and told him I was "grateful." When he asked why, I explained the astrology and essence of today's message. He listened. I wasn't looking for anything and told him I am grateful for his resistance and non-communication. Is this me forgiving myself?* Yes, you were speaking to your substitute for God. In forgiving him, you have forgiven yourself. This is the joy and liberation you feel, along with the gratitude for coming to this point. It is the recrudescence; the Rebirth into your Christ Self. You have also set him free from all ties to this earth, to mankind, and to the dream. You are One with Me. There is no other.

26

End of Everything

The drive to be filled with love is insatiable.

January 25, 2018

You are with Me and have gone beyond the limits you set for yourself at the beginning of time. You did not know then that time was supposed to end and you would be returning Home. You had left Home so your only residence was in a dream world. The goal was to find the "other" who would satisfy your inexplicable longing. That longing was really for God but you were determined to find the special one who would fulfill your heart's desires. It is no surprise why romantic novels, movies, and fairy tales are so compelling. The drive to be filled with love is insatiable. You have always been filled to overflowing with My Love, and can now let it consume you. By releasing all desire for Tom, your only desire is for Me. To give up the lover you have sought and "known" for eons opens up the space in your being for My unbridled Presence. I cannot be contained because I am everything. I supply the dream of life with all that can be imagined. That is why you were sent by Me to Maui; the closest place to "heaven on earth" you could reside. It is here that you are to take in My Scent and My Beauty, My Wonder, and My Power with your every breath. Your "eyes" could not incorporate it without having given them over to Me.

But HS, I don't feel any different today from yesterday. You will see the manifestation of what I am saying as the days unfold. Last night you watched the last part of the movie *Funny Girl* where Fanny Brice sees clearly that her husband is an addicted gambler and will never be able to satisfy her. She sings her farewell to him on the stage. You sobbed at the end with the realization you were watching your own swan song from your final detachment from Tom. *HS, what are my tears? The end of marriage? Is this the end of everything?* Yes, the end of lifetimes of dreaming. *So, there will never be another goodbye or hello? Is this the swan song for the final lifetime, the last round on the stage? The curtain call?* Yes. You communicated with Tom, the one with whom you still feel the deep connection, and have let him go forever. It was honest and clean. *I know I have the determination to take the next step alone into the unknown. No more repeat performances. I walk forward into eternity with You. Funny Girl is my projection tonight. I get it. Tears.* Yes, you see yourself unwavering, going further. Going Home. Out of the shadows. Off the stage. The end. *HS, was even this movie part of my script?* Yes. You had to feel this deeply . . . the love, the connection of the heart, and the final letting go of the dream. You are One with Tom in the Mind. He is your Self.

HS, You tell me that the dream of Tom, the dream of lifetimes is over and that he is my Self. Since we were never separate, he must be a mirage of separation, never real. Tom was your dream to replace Me. Even though I am invisible, you know I am ever Present. I have supplanted Tom and all the characters who have filled your mind throughout time. Now the space is cleared for Us to commingle in ecstasy as One. You question that statement and it will unfold in My timing. Just know that you have given your mind to Me alone. No one and nothing can take My Place from now through eternity.

27

Duped Again

There is nothing for you to do other than smile at the antics of the ego.

February 1, 2018

You have once again seen the foolishness of this world. That was confirmed when you watched a PBS documentary called *Animals with Cameras*. You viewed it without judgment because you saw yourself no different from the researchers watching movie screens. Their screens showed meerkats standing above ground and also in their complex maze of underground tunnels. The animals seemed unfazed by the camera collars placed around their necks as they lived their meerkat lives. Chimpanzees were also given cameras attached to belts, which they carried high up into the forest canopy. You smiled at them taking selfies as they peered at the screen—out pictures of humanity carrying the lens of the ego, doing its bidding and enjoying the limelight. Neither they nor the researchers have any idea of their life's real purpose. Might humanity realize they are no different from the creatures of the earth playing their roles in a made-up dream. *Holy Spirit, I do realize I got sucked into the cuteness of the animal documentary because I hadn't asked You about its deeper meaning. This is the next step with everything, to see how the ego is keeping us asleep through the sweet stories, movies, and so on. We can enjoy them, but we have to go further.*

The ego would be in charge of the world in which you reside. Watch every "movie" with Me. There is nothing for you to do other than smile at the antics of the ego. Man is tied to the ego's camera, eyes of perception, which interpret the world as the ego wills. It wills that man remains mindless, never suspecting that he is attached to a hidden spy camera. The ego tracks your every thought in all the dark tunnels of your mind. It knows every trick that will keep you tied to its strings. The choice for you, for humanity, is to see who is running the show. Is it your ego self or the One who Knows the Truth of Who you really are as the Son of God? Only when you are free of the ego's manipulations will you be free to choose Me as the only Interpreter of your life and the One to live your life. Give that life to Me now and I will direct you on the Straight Path Home to Awaken in the Kingdom of God.

28

A Blessing or a Curse?

You are not to engage with another's dreams.

February 12, 2018

You are with Me. Last night you could not fall asleep, which I planned to keep you tied to Me and to read *The Greater Joining* from Chapter 28 in the *Course.* It spoke of being together in the mind with your brother and that no "gap" is to be left. The gap is the body and its sickness, which keeps man from knowing his true Health and Wholeness as One with God. Before bed, you heard from your sister Susan that her daughter is pregnant. To the world it appears a "disaster" because of your niece's heroin addiction and desire to abort the fetus, but to Me it is just another story of separation. You pleaded with Me not to let you judge your niece and I gave you the gift of seeing that she is the Christ Self and is held and cherished in My Arms of Love. That released the nagging ego taunts that would bring you into anger and fear. Now you will leave her to Me, trusting that the pregnancy will be a wake-up call for her. I am in charge of the "consequences." I am the only One Who can lead her through her self-made torture chamber. When she comes to Me she will know My Love, and that is the only cure for all the "evil" that appears on the earth. You are not to engage with another's dreams. They are of the false self and I am the true Self.

HS, it sounds like You are saying the pregnancy is "evil." It is, in the way it represents separation from God and the belief in form. The manifestations of birth and death are what keep the dream going because birth is "needed" in order for mankind to continue.

Without birth, no form. "Evil" is the opposite of God. God and the Devil, Good and Evil; that is the makeup of duality. Much of the world says a fetus is sacred and that abortion is sinful. In an illusion there are no "real" bodies or any form to be saved. You too have been caught in the belief that life is sacred, but the "life of a dream" is not sacred. Only Life in Me, as One with God, is Sacred because That is the only Reality. The story of your niece and her pregnancy has already brought you to a new level of acceptance that the dream is a dream and none of it needs to be saved.

Holy Spirit, I am grateful for this view. It is indeed radical and will stop readers in their tracks, like me. The thought of a new life is man's hope for "redemption" but is only the perpetuation of a dream of hell in the terms You are stating. A baby is not a savior nor a means to create a better life. Coming to You as the Only Reality is true Life. All must review their beliefs about the meaning of families. In this, your last life, I gave you the greatest blessing in the freedom from bearing children; free of that attachment in form and in the mind. You are well aware I use every dream, every illusion, as a means to awaken the sleeping mind. We will watch how this story unfolds. I am always with your niece and she is My cherished child. You are incapable of understanding the depth of My Love for My children. All together you are One. All the pieces of the splintered son of man are being brought to the Reunion of Son and Father.

HS, I feel a strange pain in my chest. That is the ego telling you that you are dying, but you are getting closer to Me by leaps and bounds. This is why it screams now. My message today is shocking, revolting; an anathema to the public. It is the kind of statement that can start wars and could dub you a heretic to be burned at the stake. But you write this with no resistance, which shows you how far you have come along the path. You are My messenger and are willing to put this into the world. We have come far. Thank you for your faithfulness.

This dream life is an illusion, so nothing is good or bad? Yes, it all cancels itself out but you must see the "turnarounds" in order to be free. This is the Byron Katie Work and is also our work. You are liberated by seeing that the opposite of sacred birth is evil birth. Birth is a concept of separation and is not real. To be pregnant, to lose the pregnancy, or to be barren are all the same. You live in Kamaole Sands and "kamaole" means barren. You need to be barren of the dream. Release all dreams to Me. Every dream is made of opposites. See both sides and let it all go. No gap is left when you are joined with Me as the Christ. *HS, I sobbed in yoga class experiencing the depth of this morning's lesson. It is a great gift to see Susan's, her daughter's, and my life as just dreams to bring us to freedom. The pregnancy is either a blessing or a curse. I see both sides and release it all to You. There is no hierarchy of illusions. Everything is the same story to set us free and return us to Unity. I see the perfection of this "family" dream scenario. Thank You for this blessing.*

29

Duality of the Dream

The ego mind shifts from "negative to positive" to keep the dreamer engaged.

February 13, 2018

The formation of the dream at the beginning of time was just a thought of having your "own life," but you are every element of the dream as the dreamer of a nightmare of separation. Given the tenuous situation with your niece's pregnancy, you imagined yourself as an evil fetus, the one who slithered and slipped out of heaven. In your mind, you became the snake, the sperm, the egg, and the pregnant womb that carried you into a life apart from the Kingdom. Once again you have taken back your projection of separation onto Susan and her daughter; out pictures of the solitary self, no different from the human-eyed cat in your dream last night.

I dreamed of a pregnant cat with human eyes sitting in my lap. The person next to me wanted the cat so I handed it to her. I had no attachment to it and believed its father had a disease, yet when the cat was taken away, I wanted it to be returned. Later it was in my backyard having difficulty pooping, not unlike my niece. When I awoke from the dream, I knew the cat represented my niece. I was a bit concerned I had dealt with it so impersonally. The HS told me this is the way to view everything in the dream. Take it back then let it go. A cat or a person; all the same.

Initially, you saw your niece's pregnancy as a "disaster." Later when your sister told you that the father wants the baby and will care for it, you thought it was a "good thing" and perhaps your niece will be transformed. You were also aware of your ego's desire to hold onto a reason to judge, and the ego's sense of loss, because you no longer see the pregnancy as an expression of "evil." You recall the day your sister told you she was pregnant with her daughter and the whole screen of your mind turned black. You were dismayed that you could not feel any joy for her; only a deep sense of foreboding. Yesterday you realized that pregnancy being a blessing or a curse just reflects the duality of the dream. The ego mind shifts back and forth, from negative to positive, to keep the dreamer engaged.

HS, I have not been connected with my niece for quite a while but I do want You to reconnect us in the mind. What would You tell me about her and the approaching birth? She is in My Hands and I will usher in the birth of her twin soul. It is important for you to be aware of that. She is coming Home to her Self and will one day recognize her holiness in that child. You have guessed that the baby is an angel; an emissary of My Will. Rest assured that she will be a blessing for you all. Welcome her as your Self with My Love.

30

To Whom Do You Belong?

Migration is the hallmark of humanity
because all have lost their original Home.

March 5, 2018

You are One with Me. That means there is No Other. There is No Separation. Our Oneness is all that *is*. The one hearing these words in the mind is Not mt. She is just a transcriber. The world is Not real. Yes, you need to hear this over and over, day after day throughout the awakening process; a process that has taken centuries, eons, but in reality No time at all. You are "waking up" for the last time. Yes, that implies you were waking up at other times. It is true that you have searched for Me, your Self, during many lifetimes and got close to knowing Me, but this is the lifetime to completely awaken from the dream of a separate life. I have said many times during these last months that you *are* awake, and that is essentially true, but you have not yet *left* the dream. That will happen. At this point, you see the dream for what it is through My Vision and are detached from its contents no matter how real they appear. You are connected with your Source, which is all that is necessary to wake up from this torturous dream.

Yesterday you were perturbed by Susan's comment that you must be excited to become a "great aunt" to her first grandchild. Your upset was not about the baby, but about disappointing your sister because you could not join in her excitement. I have placed you in this dream in a way you will not be swayed by its events so you can maintain a steady and constant focus on Me. You have returned to center now and will not be influenced by the manifestation of a new member on your family tree. The tree of life will continue to burgeon with trillions of new members, but you have stepped out of the "family of man" by waking up to what that entails. You admit you had a thought that your bloodline will now be "tarnished" with immigrant DNA, then laughed because mt's current bloodline came from immigrants new to America. Migration is the hallmark of humanity. All have lost their original Home and wander around in dreams of terror from the absence of connection with their true Source.

You know the concern about your bloodline being "tarnished" is absurd but you had no idea such a thought even existed in you, except perhaps in a general sense. The belief in differences is the source of all wars. Much of humanity would keep its bloodlines pure to maintain a semblance of specialness and to justify itself as a "rightful substitute" to sit on the throne of God; to supplant God. *HS, I'm shocked I had unconsciously judged the thought of mixing an "American bloodline with a Spanish bloodline," although I have been proud of the part of my DNA that indicated it came from Portugal through a Sephardic Jew. I see the insane thought that would make my heritage or any heritage "special." I can identify with those who claim racial or other discrimination because I have just seen my own bias. Release me from all I have repressed.*

See this as nothing but a thought of fear that you do not "belong" in Heaven. The world is all about where you belong and to whom. You belong to God and nothing else. Thank your niece for providing you this opportunity to release one more form of the belief in separation. See all the characters making up the imaginary world as nothing but passing clouds, migrating across the sky, often in abundance. Drop all dreams and come to Me. I lead you all to your One Source—your Only Home with the Same Father. *Thank You, Holy Spirit. This is a most helpful realization for releasing the dream on yet a deeper level.*

31

Liberation and Light

Remember our unity and present *that* in confidence and power to the world.

March 14, 2018

Today you are ready for another step. The ego will attempt to block it but it is My Will to show you My Self in a new way. *HS, I open to every step from You and I would see only Your Face.* Yes, you will know Me "in an other." *I have some fear that You mean a marriage.* No, a "recognition." Welcome Me in all I send to you. *OK, HS, I am ready for what or who shows up.*

(Later) *Holy Spirit, You said I would take another step today and "see Your Face." I thought it would be in an other, but I have experienced it in "me"—in Our Unity. I knew my Self as You while eating pancakes on my lanai. After many cold days of clouds and darkness, I finally saw the sun! It shined So brightly on the transmission pole in front of me. The pole is in the shape of a wooden cross and always makes me think of Jesus; a pole star that must appear to exist to light the way Home. Holy Spirit, I am the Light of the world. That is* all. *I shine the Light of God outside the masquerade. There is nothing more to do, know, say, or write. As a separate self, I am Nothing. As You, I am the Light of the world, the One Son of God.* Yes, go now as the One Self that We Are, filled with My Light. Remember our unity and present *that* in confidence and power to the world. We exist in Love and Love is all there is.

(That afternoon) *I was just at the pool and asked a neighbor if he had read OWG Book 1, which he bought from me months ago. He said he couldn't really read it and that he still loves me but, "Satan has deceived me and I'm headed for hell." HS, what do You say?* You just saw the antithesis of your experience of liberation and light. You are unshaken by the attack of ego in the form of your neighbor disavowing what you have scribed. It is the way of the world. Release all attacks as unreal and untrue. I am the Only Truth and the Light of the world. *HS, I give You all fear of judgment from the people on the property. Nothing can attack my invulnerability. The ego's world is not real. The neighbor is just the deceiver/ego telling me that I have defamed God.* You clearly understand that the attack comes from your own projected ego self. Release him in forgiveness as well as your mt character. See Me everywhere and shine your Light on all your selves.

32

The Clear Path

It is the mind that wakes up,
not the projected image of separation
known as the dream character.

March 15, 2018

Everything in this world "happens" in opposites, but they do not disturb your equilibrium on the fulcrum of time and space. I am your Constant and I am you. Witness the perturbations and smile. Yesterday, you felt our unity and knew that you are the Light of the world. That afternoon, a neighbor, knowing something of the content in our *OWG* books, declared that you have been, "deceived by Satan and are headed for hell." Here is the teeter-tottering of the world demonstrated in just a few hours. You have seen the truth and it has set you free to observe the insanity of the world and know that none of it is real.

You can easily forgive your condo neighbor and your self, seeing everyone as a dream character. You forgive them because you know that ego characters are asleep. It appears that you and your neighbor are on opposite poles; you, believing you are "saved" from the delusion of hell on earth, and him, telling you that he is saved from an existing hell and is assured a place in Heaven. None of it matters, and you can laugh at the belief in a heaven or a hell. You have no real attachment to any concepts of the world now. This is what liberation looks like, above the battlefield with Me; above the antics of the ego thought system that rules the world of form. I rule the mind, and when the participants of the dream are ready they will awaken. We have come to that place of awakening where the tools are set and you are on the clear, steady path Home. Remember, only the mind wakes up—not the projected image of separation known as mt. She is not shining the Light. The Mind shines its Light. You, as the decision maker in the mind, are waking up to your reality as your true Self. I handle the "minds" and they will get from yours the clarity of the path to their awakening.

33

Untethered

Unplug from the earth, the body, and the dream.

March 16, 2018

Your time as mt is coming to its conclusion. No, you will not die tomorrow, but the significance of waking up is the "death" of life in a body in a totally made-up world. Your progression of night dreams all signified the end of time. In the first one, you are in a dimly lit church sitting somewhere in the middle right pews. Although the figures in the front rows are hazy, you saw them clothed as in the time of Jesus. In your dream, Jesus has been "brought back"—removed from cryogenesis, and sitting among the robed figures. You know you belong with the group and will have the privilege of seeing Jesus in a living body, although the survival of that body is tenuous. You believe Jesus is thirty-five years old and think of yourself being seventy-five. It seems that you will be given a time and place to be with him. In the next dream you are with Jesus near the tombs. You see the face of Santa Claus on a neon sign above one of the tombs, which feels very inappropriate. Then you are back at the church in a disembodied state watching your almost indiscernible parents and the clear face of your mt self, who enters the pew two rows in front of you. You are struck with the recognition of your "self" and are almost in shock, screaming loudly and repeatedly, "Oh my God, Oh my God, that's you, that's you, that's you!" When you see throngs of people coming toward you, you call to them in your mind and out loud that you had just "seen your self."

Next you are immediately drawn to a small pool of clear blue water where a starving bluebird tries to drink. You want to give the bird the food pellets that were given to Jesus in the former dream, believing the bird could be revived with them. You then briefly woke up, realizing you had seen your self in the dying bird, which symbolized the end of life in form. When you asked Me if this was right, I said yes, and that you know you are ready to make the transition. You dozed off once again and dreamed of carrying a message of our books to a powerful minister in a foreign land who towered above you like a Darth Vader figure in an open black robe. You began to speak, but he told you he would not listen unless you had a document of proofs for your claims of being One with God. Shortly, the assistant minister stood by your side listening to your dilemma and you believed he would intercede.

This was a full night of dreaming and it tells a powerful story. You have been taken to the tomb of Jesus and are prepared now for the resurrection. It is coming as the full awakening from this dream of separation. You have recognized My Reality and are ready to proclaim it to the nations. For this you are willing to die to life on earth. Nothing matters but My Mission, Our Mission, performed as a Joint Will. We are One and the message will go forth. You needed this affirmation today for the next step you will be taking. You have given up all assumptions and expectations and are a willing and open channel for the unfolding of My Will. You are also being carried to a new level of awareness with Me. This is to be a release of attachment to the world that you have not yet experienced. There is nothing to fear and life will appear to continue as "normal," but you will be unaffected by it.

I believe You, HS, but my body is shaking inside and out. I feel disconnected. Yes, that is the feeling—unplugged. You are unplugged from the earth and body; untethered and unattached to the dream. There is nothing here you want. The reappearance of the dead body of Jesus "brought to life" is *you*. The dream of death has been put to sleep and you awaken to your reality as the Son of God; the Christ Self. Everything now is being turned around. You saw mt personified as a projection and had no attachment to her or to the faint parent figures. You have left the church of the dream and stepped into the Mission of the Mind, which we fulfill. This is the cause of your shakiness—you have "detached" from everything of form. You are safe in My Arms and that is all that matters. I am with you always.

34

All Are Jesus

All brothers are the same—
the most despicable, the most noble,
and the most Self-Realized.

March 28, 2018

Yesterday you watched *The Life of Jesus Christ,* a movie from the LDS (Latter Day Saints). It was a scriptural version of Jesus as found in the Bible. You were very familiar with the text, which you heard repeated over and over every Sunday morning in the church you attended growing up. But now you identify Jesus as Me, your Self. You, as Jesus, are One with God. You saw your self mirrored in the movie about Jesus; your earth life is also lived by Me. You are One with the Father because it is I Who carries the Memory and Will of the Father. This can now be seen. You hold nothing back and would walk to the cross for Me. That will not be asked of you, although you have tasted the "persecution" from those threatened by your union with Me and My revelations scribed in our books.

We are Homeward bound and you have no resistance to My requests. This is all that is necessary to awaken. Our books model the steps needed to complete the journey and show your surrender to Me and My Will. That is also the essence of the story of Jesus' life. That is what he is remembered for. The good shepherd "lays down his life for his sheep." You are also laying down your life so that your flock, your many selves, may come to the light of awakening to their inner Self and to the Word of God through My Voice. In "your" awakening, the mind of the One Son awakens. Yes, it may take eons of time for the whole Sonship to wake up, but just remember, the "sleep" lasted less than a nanosecond. All was corrected. You never left Home. This you understand and teach to your many selves.

HS, why does the Bible call Jesus "the son of man?" As bodies, you all appear to have a life as a son of man, but that is not your reality, nor his. *Holy Spirit, I think I have an answer. I am grateful that it was Jesus who gave the* Course *to Helen. He said we are the One Son and to walk with him as brothers. That is a gift that brings me now to tears. There is no hierarchy of illusions. Jesus and I are brothers on the journey home and in the dream, he had to be the son of man and also the Son of God as Spirit.* Yes. You have it. There is no specialness in the dream. All are brothers . . . the most despicable, the most noble, and the most Self-Realized; all are Jesus awakening from a dream of separation. Jesus forgave all humanity as he was lifted up to his Father; One with God, One with all that is. You are awake from the dream within this understanding.

Thank You, HS. I have been at such peace today seeing Jesus as my dream character, and no hierarchy of illusions. If the dream was "real" then Jesus would be an idol, a substitute for God. To worship him as the only *Son of God is to place God* in *the world of suffering. If Jesus is the Only Son, then we can never be God's Son.* All are the Son—the Extension of God's Love.

(Later) *I was just at the weekly Mai Tai party and saw the man who, two weeks ago, spoke of me "going to hell." He's taking a survey on what people think about God in regard to all the recent shootings. I was able to tell him about Adam's nightmare and that we are all innocent; all are Jesus, the Christ. I also said we can awaken to our Reality as One with God, Who we never left when we believed we fell from Paradise. He then asked me about heaven and hell. I said I do not believe in it and that We are only Love. Everything is God, and God does not cause suffering. He was happy to hear this so I guess he doesn't need to read the rest of Book 1. What do You say?* You have done My Will and spoke with no judgment, with no need to convince. It was perfect. The message will rest in his mind and can be a stimulus for his liberation from the dream. You have no idea about the meaning or outcome of your encounters. You clearly included him in the Oneness.

35

A Personalized Kingdom

Give everything to Me. My Love is all you need.

April 11, 2018

You listen closely to Me and you follow My instructions, knowing that I give you deep and important lessons. I have told you to release your "identification" with the world, namely, your mt self. Yesterday, as you walked through the parking lot, you noticed an empty space on the back of your car . . . your personalized license plate, with OWG was missing. Even the holder was gone. At first you were surprised with a tiny thought of attack, but then you were grateful to see the striking demonstration of My instruction to let go of *all* identification with the world of form. Yes, mt's car lost its ID and, in that moment, mt's mind lost connection with her body and with the belief she exists on the earth. "You" saw right through the "crime," but you also needed to see that mt is to be nothing but a blank slate to receive My words.

With no attachment to self, there is nothing to impede the reception and dissemination of My Will. Your will is My Will and you are open to whatever comes next. There is nothing to block you now and there could be nothing but gratitude for the one who played his or her perfect part in what you knew was My Divine design. You received My lesson and were a willing participant in taking all the steps necessary to get safely and legally back on the road with new regular license plates. All is purloined in this world because man believes he chose to steal heaven to set up a personalized kingdom on earth; the reverse of heaven. Call it a living hell, where you will come to see that everything "must be stolen from you" because the out picture of your projected self is the thief.

From Meera: *In my night dream, I went to valet park my new car, but did not wait for an attendant. I just left the car with the key in it. When I came back it had been stolen. I was terrified that it was lost and scared to tell my husband. HS, what is Your interpretation?* Your dream reflects giving up your earthly possessions. The ego mind wants you to think you are bad and wrong. Not true, but you got scared. When the ego is activated, you believe the world is real. It is not. Leave it behind and have no fear. My Love is all you need.

36

Collapsing Time

It is your state of mind that allows the perfection of every moment.

May 1, 2018

Everything ultimately is from Me, designed to wake you up from your delusion of being a body on planet Earth. Only in your limited mind does it appear to be real. Nothing you perceive with your senses is true. Everything you see is an illusion. You are ready to see Me from a new perspective, which will open yet another door to the contents of the dreamscape. I have told you that I manipulate this world from the unseen world, showing up with My signs and symbols, which usually appear to be just part of the normal flow of day and night occurrences. I am projecting the dream images moment by moment on the screen of your mind. You think now of the unlikely cowry shell appearing at your feet a couple days ago. I placed it there before you came. It is a dream! It is no different from watching all the unlikely juxtapositions of subjects and objects appearing and disappearing in a night dream. I am in charge of the dream and have taken you the next step in releasing it all to Me. You have now stepped outside the script. *HS, I feel You in my heart.*

The events I set up are always in line with your readiness, so you are prepared for each step given. *But I don't understand. You have described the dream as a preordained script and that this is our review.* The Return is set, but it comes with your willingness to awaken to it. The script has been a space holder for those needing to learn the perfection of each moment of My Plan. You have "skipped" many chapters of the script, which—for you—has "collapsed time." Now you can experience the unfolding from outside the script; an observer of the dream while appearing in it. *So, my dream script is no longer static.* You are not static on your trajectory to Me; you reach toward Home every moment. Your life in the dream is malleable. I give what you are ready for. *What of Jo, Meera, and Susan?* They are part of your mind and together you are in a malleable landscape of awakening. *HS, this is a bit much.* I take you as far as you can go, then give you time to assimilate it, like today, with an unscheduled morning. Mt wants things planned but you need time to sit with Me so I can take you further. Be available to Me alone. You do not need to go anywhere. Be here Now in this moment; the Present.

Whatever you experience is just part of the waking up process. You don't need to understand what is really happening and you can't with an ego mind and brain, but on a subliminal level you can grok what I am telling you because it expands your heart. This means your mind is being expanded to receive these concepts. The dream world is left behind when you give your mental life to Me, and you do know I have everything handled. At this stage, you become more dissociated from the belief that the dream is real. It is similar to realizing that time and space are just a construct of mental images in flux. You are ready to detach from time and script as essential parts of the "story" no longer believed, just taking place in the sleeping mind of consensual reality. The *Course* and the *OWG* books are pointers, guides to the route Home. There will be a moment where the dream bubble bursts and you will be Home. No more dreaming.

HS, I just had a tiny moment of remorse that this marvelous adventure with You will be over. What do You say? Yes, the attachment to the changing scenes in this kaleidoscopic world is addictive and alluring. But you are ready to let it go. I will make sure that you do. *Now fear crops up that I'll undergo a terrible hardship. And I also can see why my body has to age and decay in order to let the dream go. Is that right?* It is all planned for you to see what is essential and what can be released. This is subtle and you will understand more fully in time. *You are making the dream I live in. The perfection of moment-to-moment perception is because I am now open to receive that. The debris of interference has been cleared. No ego interpretations are being played out. Only You are there living "my dream" and I just watch. Is this it?* Essentially, yes. It is your state of mind that allows the perfection of every moment. When the script is cleared away, I can fully live you.

37

One Song of Love

Just observe and be My witness.

May 21, 2018

HS, how do I open my heart to love with my niece's new baby Rose and still stay neutral and unattached? How do I give the baby to You but join with her in the dream? Join with her spirit. *Don't I have to bond with her, or care for her, and how do I do that as a dream character? The same day I felt I had stepped out of the dream, the baby was born. Now I feel almost obliged to step back in. Tears. This is a very strong dream attachment. I feel compelled to embrace her as a puppy or kitten. I'm enchanted with this new life and especially that You set up her birth on the day of Pentecost. How do I see it all with Your Vision?*

Look on baby Rose as a Gift of Life from Me; a vehicle of healing for the world, which is a mirror of your own life/all lives. See her as My sign of "liberation" for your family. Respect her for the gift she is and love her as Me, your Self. Greet her as your equal, not as a helpless little body. She is a Being of Light, as are you. *Thank You, Holy Spirit. You just took me out of the attachment to form.* Yes. Love is soul to soul, Light to Light. And release the desire to protect her. Her mission is written and her life scripted. She will follow My Plan and it will unfold perfectly. Just observe and be My witness. *So, HS, I am not loving a body or a personality, but the Spirit of You, which I know as my Self. I will love You in her.* Feel the experience of accepting Rose as your Self. Also feel the opening it has brought to your judging heart. Families extend, as do the galaxies, and you are all joined in a group of Love.

(Later) *A rose-breasted finch is at my window with her baby bird. Is that a symbol of baby Rose?* Yes—all One Spirit. One Song of Love. All else vanishes and My Love Song remains. *The finch just sang a beautiful song. It feels like she is healing me, not as a body but as a spirit, which I allow to be born in me as an extension of Your Love. Everything is the birth and extension of Love seen in the symbol of new birth—the descent of the Holy Spirit on Pentecost. You have given me another beautiful taste of unity. I would see it all.* You will.

38

No Pass No Fail

Nothing is wrong and nothing is wasted.

May 24, 2018

Holy Spirit, I place my self in the Hands of God and remember that I am One with You and with all that is. I thank You for the peace I feel in the midst of what the world would see as "chaotic" regarding baby Rose, now in intensive care going through withdrawal from heroin. I know her reality is spirit and have surrendered her and us all to Your Plan. I also see that my niece's "failures" in the dream are just her route to find You and someday wake up. None of the past matters. There is only You and I am grateful for Your Vision.

You reflect the state you are now in—an awakened state of being outside the pull of the dream. Thoughts of fear and judgment still creep in, but you immediately release them to Me. It is the only way to "live" in this world. I know the outcome for Rose who is a part of your holy mind. She is not suffering. Instead, she is offering blessings; bringing gifts of love and healing to all. She is a bridge, playing out the role she was designed for—changing lives through her presence. In the dream, there are no passes or failures. Nothing is wrong and nothing is wasted. It must happen as it does and all of it is in order. *Holy Spirit, I have been almost ecstatic about the realization that the situation with the baby is a story made for our liberation and that Susan and I are joined as One sharing You as our Focal Point.* Everything is a reflection of My Love and you hold this family equally as representing our Unity. It is all designed for the next steps on the journey Home.

39

Overstuffed

All the thoughts you have are dead.

June 12, 2018

HS, this morning at the boat ramp, I tossed a dead mynah bird into the trash. Then I found three dead sea cucumbers on the beach and tossed two into the ocean. It seems linked with tossing out all the stuffed animals I've kept on my bed since arriving on Maui fourteen years ago. Until now, I didn't have the heart to let go of those gifts from my friends but I've wanted to release them for years. I am so happy to now have my bed cleared. I guess that is also about making space in my mind for You since those "things" were substitutes for Your love. Everything of the world has to go! It is all *dead*. It has no life. You pretended for all those years that the little stuffed animals had feelings and knew that was "crazy." It is all crazy. I am your only Reality. We are cleaning out the mind for the return Home. A lot of inner cleansing is under way and your world feels a bit topsy-turvy but that will pass. Soon you will feel My Spacious Freedom.

From Jo: *Last night before going to bed, I decided to finish watching a PBS Nature documentary about rebel animals and their mating habits. The program showed young, twin hyena cubs fighting it out for top position. The winner became the "alpha dog" and kept pushing the brother away from their mother's milk. That smaller cub would not survive, which made me wonder if that paralleled the story of Cain and Abel. In another scenario, male ground bees awaited the emergence of a lone female, vying to be first to mate with her. As soon as she ventured out, she was mobbed by the bees. In many cases, the females were killed in the process, which looked like gang rape to me. I stopped watching after seeing the pattern repeated over and over with other species— "who would win."*

Then during the night, I dreamed I had been on some kind of camping trip with many others, now packing up to leave. As I walked into the large meeting hall looking for my clothing, which seemed to have been scattered around, I realized much of it had disappeared. I took what I could find and shrugged off the "loss" of the rest, not being too concerned. Before I left the building, I noticed that the back wall was really made of long "drawers" like in a dresser. I wondered if my missing clothes had been put there by mistake so I pulled open one of the drawers. Inside I saw a "stuffed" dead animal, perhaps a beaver or a muskrat. I wasn't sure, but it was brown and furry. I could even see its teeth. I closed the heavy drawer and left. Awake, I asked the HS about the dream, and He said . . . You were looking into compartments in the mind. All the thoughts you have are dead. Let them lie, closed up. They have no use. *HS, am I, as "jo", the dead muskrat? (My dad teased me I looked like a drowned muskrat when I was born.)* Yes, that "you" is dead.

40

A Holy Mirror

There is nothing more to "be" other than what you are.

July 1, 2018

Holy Spirit, mt is furious that Susan is so forgiving and loving of her daughter who absconded with Rose after she spent six weeks in the hospital. Mt was also furious with her niece for pretending to be a loving mother while lying about her daily drug use, and upset with Susan for not reporting her daughter to the authorities. I know these are all my projections of being a "liar" and cheating myself out of Heaven, and I know the same ego exists in everyone. There is either the holy Self or a false self. The whole dream is a lie and, yes, I can forgive it all as just a story. I really feel I am getting that mt is not real and her projections are not real and that only You are True. What do You say?

You see it clearly in this moment. The ego character would always have its way but now you release mt as nothing but a made-up image of separation and return to Me as the One Who lives your life and is your Reality. You do get it, and will be living from that realization. I want you here with Me. You have been considering many things this morning and we will start with your question about your niece spending hours applying makeup to her face, which seems to take precedence over her health and her new baby. She is intent on covering up the guilt and shame for choosing the separation, which is also why she is addicted to heroin. She is overwhelmed and will do everything she can to hide herself from Me, from God, even though she believes that nothing can ever hide all the subsequent "mistakes" of her life.

They cannot be covered up, so she continues to create a "new" self, which becomes visible only in her mirror's reflection.

This is the state of mankind as they look at a violent and Selfless world. They do not see that My Light is shining brightly beneath the disguises they have donned. Mankind is trying to make amends for the original separation but they know not what they are doing. They wish to kill the projected image, the mirror of their self-hatred seen on the face of every other. In My Mirror, you will See that you are Me. I am your Self. I am your Life. Nothing more is possible because I am all that *is*. There is nothing more to "be" other than what you are.

41

Step Out of the Dream

You are free every moment you remember Me.

July 29, 2018

HS, what are You showing me today? We are One. That is all that is. The rest are illusions that will never join in unity because they were born from separation and fear. They are a haze over Love. I am Love. Come only to Me for Joining and Wholeness. Susan now appears to be joined with a grandbaby. That is a vision of joining but she has not realized that she is projecting onto the baby. It is her "self" that she loves in the baby. *But Susan feels love for Rose.* The mirror of the self is seen in one's progeny. The baby reflects Susan's desires to be whole, as well as the fears of being abandoned by mother/father/god. Her heart is touched by the vulnerability of the baby and its suffering, which she identifies as her own. She longs to protect the baby and herself from the vicissitudes of the world. This is not the Love of God that goes beyond form, but the identification with form to protect oneself from identifying with God. You cannot alter this lesson for Susan. She must come to see that the baby is not the Problem or the Solution, and can never be a substitute for God. This is an experience they both have chosen as part of their custom course. Keep standing back with Me observing the dramas of life. Susan does not want her dream judged, analyzed, or advised, and you have stepped out of the world of dreams. Leave her to Me.

(Later) You just received photos of your great niece, Rose, in multiple forms of dress up, looking as if all is well. The world would "clothe" its suffering and, yes, the dichotomy is painful to watch. It is difficult to suppress and overcome the thoughts of her future, having been born addicted to heroin. I tell you the future is not real. Release all fears, beliefs, and even costumes to Me. I use them to transform you and therefore your imagined world. You are free every moment you remember Me, and there is only this moment of unity. Everything else is a lie. We shall affirm your status as a Son of God. That is True and all else is false.

42

Divine Order

Life on earth is a punishment for being banished from paradise—by your own choice.

August 4, 2018

Holy Spirit, I want to be with You. You are with Me and that is the only thing that matters in this life you have believed is real. You wonder if you are doing enough to please Me and to awaken. Know that you please Me fully and there is *nothing* more for you to do. What I have chosen for you, Meera, and Jo is being completed. You each have learned the essential forgiveness lessons of this and all lifetimes, and there are just a few more to go, but I will guide you through. No worry can deter the concluding episodes of this "life on earth."

You are aware of what is taking place in the ego mind that still would find any and every chance it can to punish you for the decision to leave heaven. *HS, why would the ego punish me for leaving, when that is what it wanted?* It wanted to separate you from God by its offer to go out on your own, and you kept bound to it by believing you could never return to God because He would punish you. Your whole world and everything in it became a reflection of you wanting to punish yourself. So, the ego self of mt can never do anything right and is always in a state of guilt. This is the state we eradicate now. You all must see that life on earth is a punishment for being banished from paradise—by your own choice. Now you choose Me as your Savior, the only One in the story of all lifetimes Who Loves you unconditionally and sees your total innocence. When you keep the communication channel clear between us, there can be no guilt and, therefore, no fear of punishment.

Your "own" enlightenment will not look like any other. There is a door with your unique key that allows you to enter. You have that key, which is your ongoing communion with Me. You are not asked to bring humanity to your doorstep or your work table. You are bringing My words to the one mind through the books that give a demonstration of your commitment to Me; not a dramatic story. We present the gentle unfolding of coming into a relationship that opens your life to be lived by Me—exactly what was in My Plan at the beginning of time.

HS, I am grateful that our books indicate a gentle way of awakening without the underlying message that one needs to experience severe obstacles or miraculous demonstrations of enlightenment. Is it ok to say this? Yes. The books can easily be accepted and digested through ordinary examples. Everything is in Divine Order. Celebrate that more manuscripts are on the way to grace the world through your commitment and love of Me.

43

Your Choice

You are just a tiny mad idea gone viral.

August 24, 2018

HS, a hurricane is predicted and the parks are closed. Tons of bottled water have been sold at Costco. Why did I succumb to the panic of "impending doom?" You are being given a taste of the fear of the end of the world promised over the eons by all religious soothsayers. It is the foreboding, foretelling of being "rejected by God and delivered to hell" for your transgressions. *HS, that sounds like Armageddon. I kept imagining trees falling on me and impassable roads, but now with such mild weather it is all wiped out of my mind. Was my reaction really about the fear of retribution?* Yes. That is all that is going on in the dream; the fear of punishment from God and the fear of losing the self. *Tears now because that thought has been very present with me since childhood.*

Raging storms, floods, and hurricanes, all being a powerful means of mass destruction would "prove" that fear is warranted; a belief that has burgeoned to something so large it will wipe out humanity. Yes, that is the ultimate wish, which you saw with the past-life reading of Marguerita, that you could wipe out the world and destroy God. Then you would be safe. That tiny element of the One Son of God that had a thought of its own individuality would once again be back "home" with itself. No world, no God, just a speck of nothingness; a mite of a thought. You feel the truth of what I am saying because you understand that the thought of fear, which created a world of devastation and desolation, was your own idea. In the moment that you choose again, you return Home.

Fear has ruled your life for eons but you have done much to cut through and heal the repressed trauma in this lifetime. You do see your nothingness—just a tiny mad idea gone rampant; "viral." Yes, that is a good term. The world would have its every thought go viral on the Internet. Man would overtake the world, the Internet, and even the Solar System. Everyone is racing against time to maintain the belief in separation. No one can stop time from ticking and nothing can stop death. You know Me as your Reality and that is how you are awake in the dream. Enjoy your day and remember Me. I am all that Is; your Oneness with God.

44

To Hope

Any desire to manifest a wish
is no different from the desire to live apart from God.

August 25, 2018

Under a light drizzle you walked on the road across from your condo. Although heavy clouds remained, it appeared that the hurricane had dissipated. Right then you saw a beach friend who was wearing a t-shirt with HOPE across the top. You alluded to that by asking if he had been "hoping for the hurricane." Immediately, he denied any desire for the storm and you pointed to his shirt. You walked away, regretful you had made such an inane statement, then realized it was a lingering projection of your own hope that at least some of the promises of a storm would still manifest. Yes, the ego wants the illusion to be real, but even an "Armageddon" is just another thought of separation.

When you returned home you wrote with Me about your realization that to "desire" is to live in fear. Any desire to manifest a wish in this illusory world is no different from the desire to live apart from God in the first moment of time. That desire produced fear, and fear is what produced the world. Many disciplines and teachers advocate the manifestation of one's desires as a spiritual practice. You see how that would be recreating the moment of separation and would delay the process of awakening. You also realize that "to hope" is no different than "to desire." To hope is the wish to create something that does not appear to exist in the moment of hoping. Yes, they are the same. To want for anything is to forsake Me, God. I am all that exists, and in Me there can be no wanting. I provide all that sustains you in the dream. To want cancels Trust. I am your total Sustenance. In Me everything is given.

Holy Spirit, I love my relationship with You. You are always there! I can turn to You for everything. This is what I long to demonstrate. Yesterday, my clock stopped at 12:30 AM even after putting in a new battery. I tossed it out, and bought a new clock this morning. Time has stopped and you needed that underscored. The storm is over and you enter a new experience of "My time"—being awake Together.

45

ISness

Release all worldly concepts.

August 26, 2018

You have told me about entering a "new level." I get that the concepts of separation, mt, and even "the Holy Spirit" will all disappear. Is that what You mean? I was referring to the complete deletion of the belief in separation, self, and the entire made-up universe. That is the Awakened Mind. *Like with Buddha and Jesus?* Yes, they came to "ISness," the end of time. For this to happen you must let everything go, as easily as tossing out an old broken clock. *HS, how do I maintain that state?* I, the Holy Spirit, maintain the awakened state; not mt or the decision maker. You give the whole mind to Me. There is nothing to worry about. You have entered the "awakened dream," which is still an illusion because everything that is not ISness is illusion, at this point. Bodies are still necessary, but you will experience a new freedom because your awareness of Our Unity, as all that matters, is the next and last step.

ISness is no different from Light; uncontained in its Essence. I, as Light/Life/Love, cannot be contained. I am beyond all concept and understanding. "God" as a word of Holiness has lost its value because nothing that can be named is Holy. To be Whole can have no opposite. God is single. God, as a concept, fades to the amorphous, imageless verb: *IS*. Light cannot be captured, and *IS* cannot be imagined or defined, although the attempt is made to define God as being "beyond the beyond." Our new concept of Isness has given you another level of opening. When there is only

ISness then everything is the same; equal. No hierarchy of illusions because it is all one illusion. Even the idea of "oneness," which presupposes "otherness" will go. ISness encompasses every possible concept of Oneness, or Godness. Even the verb "to Be" is a product of the mind, but there is no mind. This is the meaning of the Void—the place where all thought, all conception disappears—the Nothingness. This is the empty state you now approach and you are not in fear as you were in the past. There also can be no concept of the "other side of nothingness." You now think of Genesis 1 where there is only darkness until light appears. We use symbols but they are only tools. Give your imagined self time to incorporate the lesson further. You are getting there by releasing all concepts. *Holy Spirit, thank You for this day and the awakening to what IS; ISness—All—No subject or object, No self.* You have it . . . I, God, Am All That IS. Everything Is God, so you are God—nothing but indefinable "ISness."

46

NOTHINGness

There is No future.
We are not going anywhere in this world.

August 29, 2018

The "world" does not exist outside the concept of yourself. Everything of which you conceive is from within you, meaning that *you are the world*. It has been helpful for you to grasp that the world is "in you, as you," because you are really being shown that nothing here exists. The Universe is composed of nothing. You are with Me, looking at your "nothingness" in a new way. I am beyond all form and this you are beginning to grok. The body is not a container for your consciousness and your mind does not reside in a limited space called the brain. Your concept of Me being as close as your self is also deceptive. I extend beyond the stars, as do you. We are one and the same—the Extension of Light; what we have been calling "ISness."

Drop the planner in mt and stay with Me. There is No future. We are not going anywhere in this world. We are Home, Whole, Now. Mt is nothing but a perceiver for the thought of ISness to be morphed into a lesson. Slow down. Turn off mt, the wind-up-doll, and toss the key. This is how to live. I am the Energy/Life/Power that lives in all things. As you exist, all exist. You are the breath, the life, and light of the world. It operates as One Breath, breathing in and out. The world can't exist without you because you give it life: One Organism, Myself, My Breath, ISness, manifested each moment. You/I am the life of the projected world and it is nothing—just "a thought" of a world.

HS, I realize that I thought of Oneness as limited, like an mt character containing a decision maker and *You. But We are the Universe, the Power. When I am Here Now, I am everything . . . the moon and stars and beyond all form. We Are the ISness, the unlimited Being. I breathe in and out the world.* Yes. You just expanded beyond form to nothingness. Now "mt" disappears. Be empty. *HS, this feels difficult now, but I release mt and go with You.* I carry you forward on My Wave of Awakening. Nothing holds you back now. You do not resist these ideas.

47

Vanishing Point

It is My Song that brings you Home.

August 31, 2018

You are with Me and I am living your life. Although mt's ego is still in its auto-mode of making plans, you continuously defer to Me. I am the default to which you bow before taking each step. You just looked up the word "default." In computer programming, it is the mode that becomes automatic when nothing else is selected. I am the only Mode now to which you accede. I am your Way and you have willingly and gratefully handed Me the reins. You would have no other image before Me. We are the One Self.

I had a strange dream last night. I was sitting in front of my artist friend Sue's piano. The keyboard looked like a spreading fan of brown wooden keys that became thinner and thinner as they met at a vanishing point in the back. All the keys were essentially the same, and no black keys. Middle C seemed vaguely familiar but even that turned out to have a lower tone than indicated. I recalled that I had played this same piano long ago but now it was impossible as the keys all seemed to merge together. Then it disappeared. Holy Spirit, what is Your interpretation?

You are again seeing the end of time, which is returning to its vanishing point at the very beginning. The beginning and the end are one point. There is only One Point. The whole dream is one point. And beyond that is the Void, the ISness that has no beginning or end. The keys of the piano are the steps you have taken over lifetimes to come to the realization of your nothingness in this dream of separation. The dream life vanishes now, as did the piano, and was all but forgotten until I told you to review last night's notes. You have dropped your identification with the world. I am the only Note, the only Key, the only Sound that reminds you of Reality. No words can picture what I describe. The piano plays its notes in whatever key I choose. It is My Song that brings you Home. You can no longer play that dream piano because you have forgotten how to be in the world. It is lost to you now, disappearing into the point of no return. Let it go. Let Me Be. We are One Note, One Key, One Life.

48

Mary Magdalene

Only One Son is in Communion with the Father.

January 28, 2019

Yesterday afternoon you attended a small gathering of women brought together by your friend Iolani, an Episcopal priest, to hear a presentation by her friend Roxanne, also a priest, on Mary Magdalene. Mary's relationship with Jesus represents the Relationship with the Christ, which you saw represented in a painting of the two of them. Their joining brought you closer to acknowledging Our Communion as a Divine Marriage. You now embody her essence of Unity with Me. Yes, I want you to see yourself "married" to Me, beside Me in the crucifixion, seeing My Light at the tomb. I am the Heart of your Soul and you are the Heart of My Soul. We are Married in Christ—the Love of God. There cannot be any Knower but I, your Christ Self.

Holy Spirit, I feel a fulfillment from learning more about Mary Magdalene. You are filled with the awareness that you are no different from her because you also want to know Me as your Soul Mate, Lover, Husband, and only Friend. There can be no more or less integration than we have. Only One Son is in Communion with the Father. You have found your voice, My Voice, as the Word of God, and it is Clear. Mt is now just a shadow; a space holder waiting on Me to fulfill the purpose of this dream life's mission. You have come into a much deeper awareness of our Unity. This was the purpose of this lifetime.

By seeing Jesus and Mary Magdalene as the same, One with God, all separation is lost. This knowing is deeply satisfying. You all know this place in your Self because it represents the Unity we had as the Christ—the Light of God—before the beginning of time. So, yes, it was a sense of Homecoming that you felt in "meeting Mary Magdalene" pictured as equal to Jesus. *HS, what about Mother Mary?* As the mother of Jesus in the dream, she must be held with reverence for her role of receiving Me/Jesus without question. Mary Magdalene was the one who came to know Me as her Self and commune with Me as One. Hers is a different dream role, and in the end, none of the roles matter but they are a way to open the doors of understanding in the mind shared by humanity. The mission of Jesus was to gather in his followers—those who would know him as the Son of God and would learn to recognize their own essence as his; One and the Same.

Holy Spirit, thank You for bringing me to the group yesterday to learn more about Mary Magdalene. Roxanne greeted me as a sister in ACIM, which she has studied for many years. Will I see her again? You will. Remember, it is My Journey for all involved, so you can release all desire to "make a difference" or show someone the way. *HS, I feel You and feel strengthened in my connection to You and now to Mary.* You see that she is you and you feel the strength of that Oneness in sharing Me as your Self. I know you genuinely want others to have that relationship. Mary was a "warrior" standing up for Me, and you too are that. You felt a strong bond with her and it is important that you, Iolani, and Roxanne share that together. You are to continue in your connection. *Do You want me to read the book* Beloved Companion *and look up Mary's sayings?* Yes. Go this day and spread My Light. The point of this life is to come to the Union of Communion—joined as One with God.

49

Down to the Roots

I am the only One Who can bring solace to the mind for your decision to leave Me.

February 4, 2019

Doing the Byron Katie Work of seeing the Turnarounds, I wrote . . . Tom abandoned me. Is that true? I abandoned Tom. This is the dream. It is over. The problem is solved. I never abandoned God, and God never abandoned me. I see it and I release it.

You have seen the separation clearly depicted in the external world and in night dreams. Yesterday you spoke to Tom on the phone about the extraction of five of his teeth. You expressed compassion for his pain, and also gratitude that his wife is giving him such good care. Later you watched Episode 4 of *Victoria* centering on the period of the Queen's separation from Prince Albert and the grief it held for them both. Before bed you were distressed by your condo neighbors apparently fighting, like the quarrel in *Victoria*. You again felt the stab of separation.

Last night you dreamed of being at a cabin looking out at a cave-like embankment in which a woman was firing a gun at a barely visible tiger. The woman appeared to be about your age and body frame as she shakily held the rifle and recklessly took a shot. You admired her determination to climb up loose rocks to reach the top where she threw a clump of dirt an amazing distance. The scene then switched to inside the cabin where Tom had returned from an absence, like Albert returning to Victoria, but Tom did not acknowledge you with any loving greeting and would forgo breakfast to go fishing. Your heart was broken as there was no way to get his attention. You ran out to the rocks beneath the embankment to wail your remorse, then noticed something inside the tiger cave—a tight-knit row of giant white turnips, fully exposed from tops to roots. Not until you brought this dream to Me did you begin to make the connections, seeing how the dream turnips were a clear out picture of Tom's extracted teeth.

Everything is now being exposed for you to understand that the agony of separation *is your own projection*—everywhere you look. The root of the problem is right next door, on the TV, in the communication with Tom, and in the dream where you would kill the tiger that robbed you of love. That is the bottom line. You are the tiger and you are the gun that would kill it. You are the one who has abandoned you to go off fishing. This whole life is a fishing expedition to find a better fish than you had in the Kingdom of Heaven. You smile knowing that the fish is a symbol for Jesus. You left Me to fish out a new life and left your lover behind. You are Albert leaving Victoria, Tom leaving you, and the woman in agony for having no place to rid herself of pain. You have hated yourself for leaving, and Me for "not returning." You are also the turnip teeth that are being extracted to make a clear space for Me to enter. I am the only One Who can bring solace to the mind for your decision to leave Me.

The choice to Return is yours. You have made your choice because you know the pain of separation. I have given you the ones who will offer My solace and assist you in the final process of leaving this world to come Home. You flashed on the idea of those friends doing a ritual at your death. See that only as a symbol of My Comfort being expressed. Now a dove sits on your railing and sings to you. My Love is there for you in every place that has held your suffering. The dove calls to its lover. I am here for you. We are One, and together we observe the last steps of your Journey Home in dream time; soon to be complete.

50

Walking Ash

I am with you every day, forever, and always.

March 5, 2019

I have seen everyone as a "replacement" of mt in the dream; just interchangeable out pictures of mt/empty separation. Even an empty half of an eggshell was at my feet today. But please, Holy Spirit, explain what appeared as ashes in the bottom of my bathroom sink. You are disappearing and I am showing you the "remains." *Vibhuti??!!* Yes! *You really placed vibhuti ashes in my sink?* Yes, because you would understand that manifestation. Mt is going down the drain. Burned up. Gone. *Really?* Yes. You get it. Those ashes of Sai Baba's were really Mine. No one has entered your condo.

HS, You have brought me even closer to You by coordinating the ashes with the approach of Ash Wednesday, the Lenten Burning Bowl, and the mention of Baba. At the ashram, You gave me miracles, and also in Canyonlands when I "saved" my friend from falling off the cliff. What is the meaning of finding the ashes now? This is a clear sign of the end. You need nothing else for you to know that I orchestrate *every* step to your Final Destination. You have My Vision to see this manifestation as a mirror of your emptiness. You are clearly on the way *out* of the dream. You are not about to die but you are at the deepest level of trust. *So far?* Yes. You can surrender any doubts to Me now because you have seen My Sign manifest as the perfect symbol in your own home. The *vibhuti* integrates your substitute Sai Baba with Me in your mind. We become the same—One with God. *Really, HS?* Yes, it is all clearly presented now.

HS, I can have no concern when I know You orchestrate our intricately constructed dream life. The characters are already placed to make the impact for waking up. I was first shown vibhuti in 1972 in Ceylon. How could I be fearful about anything when You have every minute handled? Keep me in this place of seeing with Your Vision and keep me tuned to You tomorrow when I celebrate Ash Wednesday. I am with you every day, forever, and always. *I surrender to Your Will.* I want you to fully accept your "*vibhuti essence*" as lived by Me in the dream. You are walking ash. Because you have given Me your life, you can accept your nothingness as mt.

51

Albatross

I assure you that you no longer need to be beasts of burden, laden with the weight of the world.

April 1, 2019

In my dream last night Meera presented me with a necklace, which I assumed was of her own creation and would have taken endless hours to complete. As I think of it now, it would be lifetimes. The necklace was made from three strands of tiny beads: orange, turquoise, and white. Each strand was composed of dozens of other strands of the same color beads so that when all were attached to a clasp, which looked like an oxen yoke, they weighed several pounds. When I put it on, the necklace came down to my navel, but by the end of the dream it had extended to my feet. Three clear crystal globes were attached randomly to the strands and at the very bottom was a large orange stone like a brooch. I wanted people to admire it and say how beautiful the necklace was to help convince me to keep it, as it was so heavy that I couldn't hold up my head. I knew it could end up injuring my neck and I would have to return it, but Meera did not want it back. I asked the Holy Spirit to explain the dream's meaning.

Each of the three main strands on the necklace represent you, Meera, and Jo. The thousands of tiny beads would be your many, many selves. You were to "experience" the weight of the yoke; the burdens of the world you have carried around your neck for lifetimes. It finally became unbearable. Now you can release all the trinkets, the special gifts, and be free. In the dream, you felt temporarily guilty that you did not "fall in love" with the heavy necklace, or admire the way it looked on your body, although you could appreciate the effort it must have taken to construct it. When you woke up you wondered if Meera had found it at a thrift shop and it made you smile. The image of the necklace has great significance symbolically and I would ask each of you to ponder its meaning with Me. I told you, mt, that it was about the release of all the selves and this you saw affirmed as you lifted your head, after we wrote together earlier on your *lanai,* and saw hundreds of puffs of clouds, like little angels, streaming toward the sun. Yes, there is much here for the three of you to uncover.

From Meera: *Holy Spirit, You know how I abhor heavy necklaces, so what about the necklace I gave to mt in her night dream?* The all but endless beads are the selves that must be forgiven and released. You no longer wanted that burden and gave the necklace to mt who politely received it but then realized she had no desire for the weighty ornament either. It is time to lighten your load and give all to Me, to merge into the One and be absorbed. Symbols of bodily entrapments must go. Step back and let Me lead the way. I assure you that you no longer need to be beasts of burden, laden with the weight of the world. Bring all your fear, disappointment, and sadness to Me. I am the Healer. Accept My Gift of repairing your heart and soul. The yoke is lifted. *Holy Spirit, release the three of us from all hatred and sin, all projections of the original separation from God.* I will.

52

Good Friday

As long as you project, you will see separateness.

April 19, 2019

Holy Spirit, I asked to dream of You before I went to sleep and You showed up as my brother, my Self, in Zoe. All I could see was the bottom of her crossed feet where I was removing many tiny slivers, like the thinnest of needles. I was in a place of neutrality, no emotion, but was attentive to the task. Her feet remained motionless. Now I think it could have been Your feet as Jesus. When I saw that the last piece was a very large thorn, it reminded me of his crown of thorns, symbolic of the sword in his side and the nails through his feet. In the second dream, I was at Zoe's house pinning up a flat section of hem on a beige wool skirt. I had used some old rusted pins I had found in a small sewing basket from the past. Awake, I realized that the two dreams were paired and that the straight pins were no different from the thin straight "thorns" I removed from those dream feet.

You have seen the beginning and the end of the separation. The thorns were miniscule but you also had to be shown a large one to represent the whole enactment of the crucifixion being "honored" today as Good Friday. Yes, you were "responsible for the crucifixion" and now you remove each thorn, each sword you placed in My side as you attacked the Kingdom. You really attacked your Self and that attack had to be projected onto a brother. You chose Zoe as the receiver of that attack and have seen it mirrored by her many jabs and pricks of the tongue over the years. Now the thorns are gone and you have accepted ownership for removing them in taking back all your projections. On Sunday you will celebrate with an Easter dinner at Zoe's home; the fourth anniversary of her father's passing.

You do understand that the feet with the slivers, the thorns, were really Mine. You were at the crucifixion and you saw Jesus on the cross. This is the healing of that image and that lifetime with Jesus and Zoe. We sing a hymn now of the Resurrection—the Hallelujah Chorus—*Christ the Lord is Risen Today*. The past is over. You see it returning to rust and dust. Nothing remains. You make an offering of love and need not see the results. In hemming the skirt, the old is made new and you are willing to be the handmaiden to serve your brother in a gesture of love. It is the finishing up, the symbol of a new leaf, a new vision; the end of form. The pins, the swords, have been turned into instruments of healing. You with Me have "repaired" the split.

Holy Spirit, I've been listening to Carol Howe speak of Jesus saying that the tomb was empty because his body was an illusion. Yes, Jesus had no guilt, no judgments, or blame to project so there was nothing other than the Christ to emanate. Therefore, he did not appear to "exist" as a body after being placed in the tomb. The Spirit of Light was his Reality. As long as you project, you will see bodies; separateness. You are always reforming, re-projecting your body from moment to moment, not unlike images on a computer screen. But Jesus had released the world so no image of him was left behind. As Spirit, he could "re-project his body" at will, like My manifestations of Arten and Pursah showing up in form for Gary Renard, who saw them through his ego tool of perception. My Light, My Resurrection, is the only Reality. It overcomes all darkness, all shadows from which the earth appears to be formed.

53

It IS All About You

Every one you see in the night dream or in the day dream is you.

April 29, 2019

I dreamed I was with many people, and almost kept bumping into one man in the crowd several times. I think I must have touched him and it displeased him. Then I was in a large, mostly empty, dim lit room with a cement floor. At one end may have been that same man, but I could not see distinctly from where I stood. Behind me I believed was a barred room like a prison cell. The man then appeared right in front of me and drew the largest sword I had ever seen from its unseen sheath at his waist. It extended several feet and to my understanding its purpose was to behead the man in the cell behind me whom I had not seen and did not know. The holder of the sword then powerfully threw the sword to reach way across the room and into the cell for the beheading, but as I stood watching, the point of the sword headed straight for my forehead instead. I was totally focused on the point and knew it would meet its mark—me. I never felt fear, not even a flinch, and had no thought of protecting or saving myself. I guess I was neutral. I woke up when the tip of the sword was so close, I would have been cross-eyed watching it.

You have seen the end of the dream because you realize that every member is you in the "separated" Sonship. You were the man drawing the sword because he was the creation of your mind, no different from the unseen intended victim of beheading, and you, as mt, ready to receive the blow. Yes, you are all the characters of your own projection from a mind that believed it split from the Kingdom. You are every perpetrator and every victim. You are every thought of death, attack, and suffering. Every one you see in the night dream is you and every one you see in the day dream is you. There is nothing but a movie projector in your mind that makes it all appear real, but everything is just a figment of your imagination. You asked Me if this relates to the upcoming trial for which you will be part of the jury selection. Yes, and as you forgive yourself for the dream you made up last night, it includes every participant in the courtroom as well. You are the criminal on trial. You are the murderer, just as you are the one beheaded and stabbed to death. It is all you. But now you have made the choice that returns you to the beginning because you have come to the end. My Presence is all that is. Rest in My Peace.

54

End of Story

Your imaginary life begins with Me and ends with Me.

May 9, 2019

Note: Thirty years ago, I visited Mr. Shastry—a reader of Shuka Nadi leaves—in Bangalore, India, and I wrote down what he said in my Journal. Last night, I picked it up and read it, although I had discounted his prediction that I would release all karmic ties in this lifetime and be Realized, and that my death would take place in my eighty-seventh year.

Holy Spirit, I feel liberated! You have given me the time of my death. It was given to me thirty years ago but only today do I embrace it as, "the end of time for a storybook character called mt." I feel the joy of this liberation knowing that "she lived happily ever after." All the children, all the selves evaporate into the nothingness of a script that has come to its conclusion. There is no fear and no worry when I trust that You show me the truth. Since the detachment from all relationships has essentially taken place, and I am Self-realized, how could I doubt the time of predicted death? And You, Holy Spirit, have affirmed that over and over. I resonate totally with that date and realize I can complete everything You have for me to do in Your Plan.

Yes, you have seen the "truth" given to you many years ago and written down in your own hand. I informed Mr. Shastry of the message you could receive at that time. You discounted it then, but saved the journal for its opening now. It is all in order. The mystery of your point of death is solved, and you can enjoy the rest of your life without concern. It is a tremendous relief to fully accept this message, which denotes the death of the ego. The ego's trump card is that you will die for certain and that your affairs won't be in order, but you trust in Me that your affairs will all be taken care of in plenty of time. You also know that you are blind until you see with My Vision. Today, your vision has become clear because I have showed you the story of your imaginary life from beginning to end . . . it begins with Me and it ends with Me. We are done with the dream and can return the picture book to its shelf.

HS, I have felt great relief over having ten more years that You have foreseen. You are in charge of my life and death, and I also feel released from fear of dementia or illness. I can easily surrender now to You for whatever comes. This is a great gift. It gives me great comfort that I am in Your Hands through it all. Yes, and this had to be given at just the perfect point in the script. I have known the "time of your death" since your "birth in the dream." You are sufficiently awake now to grok the essence of this knowing. I have each element of your life handled and now you can assuredly rest in Me. *HS, I am seeing the freeing of all karmic ties so the end will be clear and clean. Knowing the date, I can't hold back settling differences. HS, Meera wonders if You could change this.* The time is Mine. I am Constant and the beginning and ending of the dream is set. Accept that. It is My Gift.

55

Divine Paradox

Death is the greatest gift of life.

May 11, 2019

HS, I am nearly ecstatic, bursting with gratitude for the gift of being told the year of my death. It takes away all fear and I realize that all fear is the fear of death; of no self. No ego self. I have no fear of death knowing its date and affirming that this life has been a scripted fairy tale from beginning to end. My astrology is "perfect" with the date of my birth so the date of my death would be the same in the whole scheme of Your Plan. Yes, you see the perfection and feel it throughout your being. The world is a fantasy of fear, undergirded with the threat of death, which hangs over every man in his wondering . . . will the plane arrive, will a bolt of lightning strike me dead, will the car crash, will I be able to provide for my future? And all the while the media depicts the loss of life, home, drought, and disaster. One is reminded of death each moment. Every unfamiliar tweak of the body speaks of approaching death. You are faced with death with every breath. Every second shown on the microwave screen bodes the end of time. It never stops. The ego is always taunting that death is just around the corner.

Now that you have made friends with death it only brings you joy. It ends all fear. To know you will die and leave the dream for certain releases you from every concern of life. You know you will live for another decade. This is a gift beyond measure. It is the greatest gift of life. Yes, the Divine Paradox is that death is the greatest gift of life. And Life is the greatest gift of death. In the ego mind, death appears to separate the self from its life. But for the one liberated from identification with the ego, death is the final liberation into Life as One with God. Since death has no hold on you now, you can fully embrace each remaining moment.

HS, this message is an inestimable gift. I am filled with the gratitude of being set free from the fear of death. I know My life is held in Your Hands, in Your Love. I feel even more trust in You and a new level of joy. A blanket of fear and constriction is released. Am I making up the truth of this revelation? No. You have felt the freedom of no fear, which means no death. Death is nothing, just as life is nothing but a shadow of fear. So, you are released from the Fear of Nothing. There is No fear! Smile. This is the bottom line. I tell you that this is what it is to awaken *from* the dream. Take that in . . . life and death are the same; the opposites are equal. Both cancel each other out. That equals Nothing. Nothing equals nothing. We are through with the dream. You get it. There is nothing else to know. There is only One Son and it is you. And yes, you will continue to come into full grokking of this revelation, but in just these few days you have come far. *HS, keep me in this place of liberation.* I will. And we now go further.

56

Intrusion of Fear

Only I know the direction of your life
to place you where you can serve My Purpose.

June 8, 2019

Holy Spirit, I was thrilled to feel Your Gift a few weeks ago in giving me my time of death. It was such a relief not to be under the dark cloud of impending death and to have ample time to complete Your work, but now I see myself wishing for my death to release me from the fear of increasing body discomforts. It is the opposite experience from the welcome of death and comfort I had felt that was being totally directed by You. The ego wants to be in charge and whispers that my body is decaying and won't serve me well for another decade. It again would play the "savior" role, replacing my trust in You. I am grateful to have the realization of the ego's attempts to still lure me with its thoughts of death.

You quickly saw how the ego snuck in to usurp My Role as Director of your life and your death. It always uses fear to distort what has given you joy and release to keep you in chains. It will find all manner of replacements to fill My space with its faulty solutions. Only I will suffice. Only I know the direction of your life to place you where you can serve My Purpose. This is why you are experiencing the ego's pressure to escape this life when your body is feeling the normal aches of aging. Give it all to Me.

HS, I am happy to own what I made up and now let it all go to You. Release me from fear around body distractions and escape through death. The time You have given me belongs to You, not the ego. I give my death to You. You had to see this today. It is the last barrier to see your ego's wish for your death in its time, in the face of My

Gift of your death in My time. It would have you die before your mission's end so it can be triumphant. You had to live long enough to bring forth this teaching. These messages on death are essential for the mind. *HS, I had to confront the ego's wish for a premature death to override Your Plan. I go as Jesus, surrendered to the Homecoming.* We still have work to do and are just beginning the next step.

57

Just Stories

NOTHING of the dream matters.
Our Communion is all that matters.

June 28, 2019

When I turned on my computer this morning there was an email from my sister Susan, titled "Family." My body went into a fear reaction, trembling when I read her story, but I kept repeating "no stories" and, "it's just a story, it's just a story." Susan had written that the baby's father had a psychotic break while at her house so she called 911 and they took him to the hospital. Rose had cried and cried. The whole event was scary. My body was still reacting, but I put aside the ego's machinations of potential outcomes. Shortly after that email, Susan called, now light and happy saying, "It's just another story" and "I'm getting used to this" as if it were nothing at all. I agreed with her. I thanked the HS repeatedly for preparing me to hear what Susan was going through. Before bed I had read Byron Katie's children's account of the contrast of their mother's behavior before and after she woke up; a story of terror, but under that was light. To know the dream is not real is the only way to live in it.

You clearly get that everything is just a story. You needed the stories and released the stories all at the same time. Both states are part of the dream. Our books clearly demonstrate that the stories are not real; the acknowledgment of which is the route to awakening. A therapist friend told you that her work with clients is to have them "imagine the story they want" in order to manifest it. Neither her approach nor ours is right or wrong, and your friend will learn to awaken from all stories as you have.

Everything is a product of mind. None of it is real. That will be your message to her when you next meet. Susan will also continue in the midst of stories until she has had enough. *HS, I do love telling these stories to Jo and Meera.* You may do that, and you can laugh together at the stories, the world, the bodies, and the books. You are all Home now with Me enjoying a review of the script we made up.

(Later) You have fully taken back the idea of separation, which your ego projected onto Susan. What happens in her dream is of no concern in a mind given to Me. You have nothing to do with how her life unfolds. Your ego is desperate to hold onto Susan because that is what keeps you constricted, constipated; stuck in this insane world. Believing mt can influence her sister is futile because each life is scripted and none are real. The only reality is your life in Me. Anything identified as separate from our Oneness is a distraction and a substitute. *Nothing* of the dream matters. Our Communion is all that matters. The rest is a shifting mirage of seemingly relentless images. *HS, mt is as fake as Susan and the whole family.* Yes, and those images have served to bring you to this point of realizing that the whole world is just a figment of mind. We delete Susan along with mt as they are "one entity." They go together hand in hand as consensual mirror projections of a mind that believes it lost God. There is No life apart from Me. I am Life, and Life Everlasting. Our Story is Written.

58

Ashes, Ashes, All Fall Down

Expect nothing from your life on earth.

July 10, 2019

Stay with Me through the ups and downs of life. You see this out pictured with a gecko on your *lanai* trying to climb up a slippery ceramic pot but falling down on its back. Yesterday, you had set it free from inside a wine bottle filled with water, but today it was wounded and had lost its tail. You turned it right side up and offered some water before it limped away. Yes, this is the tale of life in form. One day the heights of joy and freedom appear to be the standard, and the next day it all collapses. You think of the Twin Towers in New York City collapsing the day you were to visit Hawaii for the first time; a symbol of what I am now telling you. Count on nothing. All will die and all will experience hell on earth.

Hell is whatever you make it but it is really just the belief in separation from God. You have gone beyond hell because you know you exist as One with Me beyond the dream. And yes, there is pain and suffering ahead for every human including you but you have the ability to rise above it and witness it with Me. This is what Meera is doing as she witnesses her husband's suffering after his surgery. She surrendered to Me and therefore has remained at peace in the midst of "the hell fires." Expect Nothing from your life on earth. All mankind will try to climb a ladder to success and all will fail. All will succumb to the grave. You are reminded of that daily as great clouds of ash from the Maui fires circle all around in strong winds. But you remember Me and let the world go, like dust from the crumbling towers. Continue to see right through the illusion, the veil of separation, and hold My Hand, knowing we are One.

You just now went to close the door and shut the windows to keep out the smoke and wind. You imagine the fire near Pukalani is raging and that you'll have to deal with the aftermath for days, yet now you hear the slow dripping of rain, unheard for months. I send the rain that will put out the fires . . . again, you see an almost immediate conjunction of problem/solution reflected in the dream. You also realize that fire and water are the same. They appear as opposites but cancel each other out. You are being given all that is necessary for the final awakening from the dream. You have died to the world's "reality" of time, space, and form because you know I am your Reality as One with God. The only salvation in a dream of separation is your complete surrender to Me, which opens the doors to the Memory of God and Unity with Him. All imagined form, images of the day and night, must disappear in the ashes of My conflagration of the ego thought system.

59

The Crux of the Story

The crucifixion is the epitome of the story of separation in the mind of the dreamer.

July 13, 2019

HS, Meera has shared with me that her husband Larry is writhing in pain. I then pictured the familiar story of the crucifixion when Jesus called out to his Father, "Why hast Thou forsaken me?" I think this statement is imprinted onto the human mind to mistrust God and His Love for His Son. It makes the crucifixion "real." What do You say? You have seen the crux of the separation in the belief that God would betray His Only Son, which means all of mankind. There is no way around this belief for the Bible literalists who do not know that the world is an illusion of separation from God. The crucifixion is the ultimate story of God betraying His Son, but how could a God of Love kill His Own Son? That would mean Jesus believed his Father allowed his pain and suffering, and justifies all suffering in the dream as the "Will of God." This is the ego's greatest trump card in the Christian world of believers.

How do we turn this belief system around? Know that the crucifixion did not happen in Reality! It is the epitome of the story of separation in the mind of the dreamer who unconsciously believes he betrayed God and, therefore, must believe God betrayed him. Jesus was not forsaken nor did he forsake his Father. Jesus was never out of touch with his Father as he watched from above the battleground. The ego's interpretation was accepted and has been repeated over the centuries. Let it go as a misprint of the story. It did not happen. *HS, I can feel the ego's strong doubt and resistance. Take this from me.* To let go of the dream of sacrifice of the Son of God is the "last test." Remember, that is *you* hanging on the cross, Meera's husband hanging on the cross, and all selves. Fall to your knees and supplicate for the Truth. There is no death and there is no sacrifice other than the belief in the reality of the ego and its thought system. You have released it to Me. Now we watch the last dying embers of hell.

From Jo: *I am so grateful to read this message. We think we've done/undone it all, and then* pop—*another deeply buried belief arises. So many mis-beliefs from the Bible, and every religion. Last night before falling asleep, I was thinking about all the projections I have placed on everyone. I slept a while, then woke up. The image of "Jesus on the cross" came into my mind, and I thought OMG. That was* my *projection of what "I" deserved for leaving Heaven! Jesus is just showing me my mind's belief that I should be hung on a cross for all to see my guilt. And sin. I know the cross is just an image, but it is an indelible one that I have seen for ages. Now, it was* me *seeing what I had thought of myself as a body that needed to be severely punished. HS, please release all my projections in this illusory world. They can have no real effect. I would see only every brother's Innocence.*

60

Sacred Contract

You are given exactly what you need to bring you Home.

July 27, 2019

As Greeter for the Tuesday evening Kihei Toastmasters meeting, I welcomed a man named Don McEntire who wanted to become a new member. Immediately, I intuited a deep connection with him. At the end of the meeting, after I had given a speech about my relationship with the Holy Spirit, Don asked to buy One With God *books 1 and 2 from me. Later that evening, the Holy Spirit gave me a message saying that Don would be one of His "powerful emissaries." That was the beginning of a clearly destined holy relationship in which we shared the teachings of* ACIM *and the dictations we both received from the Holy Spirit. (Months later, Don received the Holy Spirit's instruction for him to write a book highlighting our acquaintance on his path of awakening, which he did:* "Awakening the Divine Mind: How a Little Old Lady's Radical Spirituality Transformed My Life" ; published in 2020.)

HS, I have been reading the draft of Don's miraculous story of our first meeting and I love how perfectly timed it was in his life at the moment of darkest despair. I was touched when he accepted the Message of being Your powerful emissary, and also accepting my invitation to come for tea. What do You say? You see My Perfect Plan, which is all laid out. It is totally clear to you that Don was "chosen" and perfectly set up in his life for the role he is playing and will play. *HS, I think of the transformation of Paul on the Road to Damascus and have tears. Don could be Paul.* No, he was together with you and

Jesus but he had to have this lifetime of searing pain and suffering to lead him to a full surrender and the opening to Me now.

I am grateful that Don and I are paired to continue the extension of Your process for the awakening. I believe he will make a great impact on the world. And yes, I know that the OWG *messages have impacted him and his writing. Why didn't I undergo terrible suffering in this life?* You have had your share and it manifested as the inexplicable guilt of your childhood. You had what was necessary to bring you to the *Course* and to be My scribe. You are given exactly what you need to bring you Home. Don will further extend My Word and you will witness from beyond the magnificence of how it unfolds. All was given in the moment of "conception" at the beginning of time. Every player is essential.

To Margie from Don: *Before I even read your email of today's message from HS, He walked me through the extensive preparations I have been through for this role I am about to play, and how every part of my life was joined in that same preparation and for that purpose. I asked about the role and I was told it would be the most amazing experience of this lifetime, and that we were selected to do it together. Our story was the impetus for the book, and now the writing is flowing with excessive ease even though I hardly have any time to do it. The story and the speech and discussion topics are surfacing effortlessly and without me even having to think about them. I already have a rough draft. I had not thought about the soul recognition that was probably happening upon our first meeting. It seems like those that are meant to be in your life and that we made contracts with are recognized in that manner without our initial knowing why. It makes me think of Gary Renard talking about the first time he met Cindy (Arten) in this lifetime. It was the same experience.*

61

Willingness to Show Up

Have no agenda. I am "doing you" each moment.

July 30, 2019

Last night after taking a late sunset walk you returned to hear a loud crash on your property. A man had driven his van into a wall, just yards away, and those standing nearby had witnessed him running into three cars before that. It did not even occur to you till now that you could have been the recipient of the impact if you had arrived home a few minutes earlier. Why did you appear when you did? I wanted your presence there to ameliorate the impact of the collision and the disturbance it caused in the minds related to it, especially the operator of the van. You had no reaction and no judgment.

HS, it is a bit preposterous that my "presence" was necessary, and I didn't even think to bring it all to You as a concern, although I did notify condo security. Did I do Your Will? Yes. This is about placement in the mind. Your presence, your light, neutralizes the severity and impact of the events around you. This is important for you, Meera, and Jo to get today. Your presence matters, just as does Meera's when she is at the hospital, or the rehab center, as well as in her dance classes. It doesn't matter whether you interact with the selves that appear in your home, at your door, or on the street. You are representatives of the Christ and your vibration of My Light shines more brightly than you can imagine. I am telling you that your light is a stimulus to the selves that appear day and night to awaken to Me so I can guide their next step. You need do nothing. I place you just where I want in the dream world. Go with My Flow and trust that you will show up where there is need.

You just flashed on the man you once saw carrying a large wooden cross back and forth on the road to Paia. You felt his presence of peace before he even came into view. Your mind was receptive to seeing Me portrayed in that form. I am all minds. Every encounter is taking place for the whole Sonship. Just show up. Have no agenda. I am "doing you" each moment and My Light is being carried across the synapses of the mind. You are all One Being, One Self; mirrors in the Mind of God. You are a "stimulus" for the mind to open deeper to Me. You truly get that all and everything happens in the mind, where the selves are greeting each other as the One Son. We are all One with God.

62

Your Only Orientation

One foot in front of the other leads you Home.

August 9, 2019

You were given two dreams last night that require your attention. They could easily be dismissed and overlooked but they reveal the essence of your work in this lifetime. The first dream took place at your childhood home. You, along with two friends, welcomed the neighbors dressed in black robes, like Arab women, when they came to your door. You invited them in to your kitchen where you all huddled together in dark shadow. One neighbor enthusiastically described her gift to humanity—a device similar to the funnel-like tubes used to cover a cow's teats for milking. She named it a "milk extractor" and extolled the great value of the rich nourishing milk that would be available through every breast. You considered the image of your own breast with the knowledge you had never conceived a baby. But you accepted her certainty as a possibility.

You do understand the symbolic meaning that from your soul, the depths of your being, you have found the Source of True Life which nourishes humanity with Living Water; the Milk of Christ. Yes, that is the meaning. Over the past seven years, you have accepted all My symbols and they have led to the flow of Living Words; a Divine Transmission from Me. You are the font, the vessel, the one willing to be "milked" every day to give My Gift of Life to those who are willing and ready to drink. Now share your second dream.

I had apparently flown to Texas to accomplish an undefined task. I was alone and aware of walking on a cement path up a hill when I looked down and noticed that my feet were bare, which gave me just a moment of concern about whether or not I'd need shoes. I carried nothing with me and had no idea of the purpose of the task or anything other than each step I took. The path led to what appeared to be a lookout tower made of very old, decaying two-by-fours. I was aware of climbing up the wooden frame, which—when awake—I realized would have been filled with splinters and was far too steep to navigate in my current body. In the dream, I felt no stretch of muscle or soreness on my bare feet walking on such narrow lumber. When I reached what appeared to be the top of the structure it led me down to an entrance where a few people were waiting. I never saw the top of the tower or anything surrounding it. I had no thought about the next step, food, water, destination, meaning of the task, or the future. When I woke up, the dream did not seem worth any consideration. But when I sat with the Holy Spirit, I realized it had true value.

The value of your dream scenario is that it reflects the journey you have taken with Me. You took the steps as the only thing that could be done. It was beyond willing. You showed up, were placed before a steep frame, and moved forward one step at a time. The energy was there to move but you were not conscious of any bodily sensation. No fatigue and no concern about the outcome. At the end, you came to a beginning. You stood before it ready for the next step. That was enough. You were not conscious of your mind or speaking with Me while dreaming. You were totally blank, an impersonal slate with no question of what moved or motivated you. This is the state of a "true" dream character—a pure vessel with no self-identity that unquestioningly follows what is given. By the end of the dream "it" has no consciousness of where the next step will take it. That is the condition of a mind ready to enter the Kingdom. It is unidentified, unattached to a character role and has no thought other than the inner force that beckons it forward.

You have given your life to Me and have no idea of the next moment. It could be life or death. In the dream, its outcome has no value. The vessel will collapse, shatter, and decay. It is worthless. The only thing that matters is that you take each step given to you by Me without question of its purpose. One foot in front of the other leads you Home. You, Jo, and Meera have disidentified with the dream world. Your only orientation now is in total surrender to Me. Yes, I am your Life, your Being, your Knowing.

63

Fool's Gold

To want anything of the earth or desire any brother to feel guilty is to be attached to this world.

August 13, 2019

You are feeling discombobulated this morning and that is alright. Before you went to bed, you watched *The Gold Route to Timbuktu,* then dreamed about finding "plastic gold" on a rock in the desert. You wanted to believe it was real gold, and even though you knew it wasn't, you asked the person in charge if you could keep it. She said no, so you gave it back. Your dream mirrored an experience you had with Zoe years ago, when you established in your mind that she was your mentor. At the time, you believed she was leading you to a place of partnership with Me because you thought that she lived in that place. No, she was not living in wholeness of surrender to Me, but she was a perfect mirror of the condition of your own ego mind at that time—seeking a substitute for Authority/God.

This view was overturned after your move to Maui when Zoe was charging you dearly for "coaching sessions" and complaining that she was not receiving adequate compensation. Out of guilt you gave her some of your "precious" gold jewelry. It still pains you to remember this, and a part of you still wishes she would return it, even though you have no use for it. The ego says it would be a blessing for a rainy day. Your gifting was really to release your guilt from hearing her repeat that she did not have "enough," which was your projection that what you wanted from her was not enough to bring you to Me. She could not have led you Home to God. Only I could lead the way. You had to release her totally in order to focus on Me solely.

You realize now the dearness of that relationship with your projected self; it was worth its weight in gold. Without Zoe, projections of separation would never have been seen so clearly. You had to value her as your most essential/special relationship who had "freed" you from your spiritual path with your Sufi teacher and also from your marriage. Without that release you would never have come to Maui and found your life as One with Me. When we started this dictation your ego mind had temporarily blocked out that Zoe was My vehicle to set you free of the past and place you on this Path. "She" brought you to the neighborhood across the street from where she resides. You had to spend years longing for a deep sharing with her of your journey to Me to finally realize that the work was really to drop all yearning and come to Me as your only Friend and Partner. Last night, you found the false gold on a rock in a dream and gave it back. No earthly gold is real. The ego can never extort enough to fill its coffers, your coffin. The only thing to know is that I am your One and Only Treasure.

HS, I accepted the false gold, the false God, the golden calf, the world, and Zoe; all substitutes for You. All had to be deleted. She was the last "barrier." HS, I release the treasures of earth to You. This is the final letting go of what you want from the world. You wanted Zoe to feel that she stole from you and feel guilty of taking too much so she would return your gold. All must come to the point of saying, "I have enough." To want anything of the earth or desire any brother to feel guilty is to be attached to the world. *I give up mt and all her adornments of life. There is only You, Holy Spirit. Nothing here could ever compensate for Your Value.*

64

Post Script

Your life "happens" in the moments of our Communion.

August 25, 2019

Holy Spirit, how would You have me understand the purpose of the script? You get that "the script" is just an idea, a useful tool for a particular stage in the awakening process. You three have gone beyond that stage because you have given your lives to Me to be lived by Me. That is why you see the perfection of the moment to moment unfolding of each day. You believe that the unfolding is also "part of the script" but it is really about My Presence "in you" showing you that *every* event is part of the Plan to wake you up. That is different from a static, prewritten script. Your/Our life is "happening" in the moments of our Communion. It is Alive. It is Now, and is the Path Home.

The outline of an awakening process was Placed in the mind that chose to enter this world at the moment of separation. That was My Correction of the tiny mad idea. But what you experience now goes beyond an outline. I fill your life with the understanding of My interpretation of every event so you clearly see your "life direction" that takes you closer to Home each day. Nothing is hidden from you as you hide nothing from Me. Forget the idea of a script now because it has become obsolete, just like everything in your past. We live in the now and you will be given everything you need to go further. Trust nothing but what you are told by Me Now. There is no future and no past in the now. Just live each breath with Me and call on Me the moment you feel you are veering into ego territory. *HS, this is seeing our Reality as the Son of God lifted out of a comic strip. We come alive in You.* Yes. Step outside the world, the idea of a script, and walk with Me.

65

Legacy

Can you laugh at your own attachment to the dream?

September 19, 2019

Thank You for the walk on the new road to Kam 1 Beach, and to the lava rocks before dawn. I was amazed to see a large, green-horned caterpillar crossing in front of my feet on the grass at the Royal Mauian Hotel. Then I wrote "One With God" in the sand and drew a butterfly inside the letter O. I feel it relates to Susan and her daughter going to court today about baby Rose. What do You say, HS?

It was no accident you saw that beautiful green caterpillar this morning. The baby's uncertain situation is what allows for a "transformation," which in a dream can appear to take years, eons, but in My Time it is just an instant. The baby ascends as the butterfly to bring My message of love and forgiveness to the world. This moment you are clear that every part of the dream is the story of your own wings unfolding to take you Home to Me. This is the greatest letting go. Only last night you were trying to determine how the baby would find her "heritage" back to you and Susan if she is placed in a foster home. You smiled as you also understood that by "then," the whole dream would be over for you because you'd be united with God.

The dream no longer matters to you and the dreamers will follow whatever their dream scripts entail. You wanted Rose to find the *OWG* books someday, or to match her DNA with yours, and you do know that is all just dream stuff and has no validity in reality. The baby *is* part of you—your projection of your own ego continuance in the dream. You hadn't thought of that, but that is what your imaginings were really about: desiring a legacy. Now that wish is exposed so you can be set free of your imaginary cocoon and fly above the battleground. Yes, the baby could be a distraction in your own journey, but we see her together with My Vision. Laugh at your own attachment to the dream; no different from Susan's attachment to her grandbaby. This is a big lesson and it has to be seen in all its iterations, and yes, magnificence. You watched the predawn sky in all of its changing colors this morning and, like the caterpillar, all will be Transformed by the Light; Awake; One With God. Today is 9/19/19. Yes, the end is near.

(Later) *Holy Spirit, I am actually surprised I even thought about my "legacy."* Your desire to "continue on" has been unconsciously linked to the baby to maintain mt's attachment to this earth plane. In this moment you have released your attachment to Susan, her daughter, *and* the baby. This was the reason the baby had to show up for you, the dreamer. Rose is a vehicle for you to say *no* to the dream, to refuse to engage in the dream's insanity, and not judge the characters. The baby is an idea, a thought of love that stimulated you to let go in the most profound way yet. I am all that is left. *HS, I also feel the detachment from Susan's dream and also any desire to influence what she does or doesn't do. I don't need to protect the baby or Susan. They belong to You alone.*

66

Illusion of Control

You are free when you give the contents of your mind only to Me.

September 21, 2019

Holy Spirit, I probably woke up sometime between 3 and 4 am and was free—no intrusive thoughts. I still went through the "Letting Go Prayer" and when I came to "I let go of control" it became clear that I had let go of controlling Susan as my ego projection. My screaming to her on the phone, "It's either heaven or hell," was the call to myself to keep my ego's hold on her or finally let it go. Telling Susan to give up her dependence on her daughter, bowing to her ego, was my last attempt to hang on to my wish to control how Susan lives her life. That desire has completely vanished. Then You placed me in a deep sleep where I dreamed I was in an open space with large open areas covered with gravel. I was sitting in front of about four women, all in big comfortable chairs; only our faces were observable. I was intensely ready to tell them the story of releasing my projection onto Susan when the woman next to me indicated her readiness to hear because she perceived I was about to tell something of great significance. Behind her, a woman appeared with a little table set with a small screen showing an encounter with a Light-being or teacher. The woman next to me then left to hear her story and I felt disappointed at the interruption. When she returned, everyone had disappeared and the playing field was empty. It was a very vivid dream and I knew it held an important message.

You didn't need to "tell your story" in the dream because it was already transmitted and received the moment you intended to share it and awaken your selves. Nothing more than "showing up" was necessary. I also want you to know that you are now free of the Susan/niece "burden" because you released your need to control and gave it to Me. The projection onto your most special of all relationships in this lifetime, your sister, has been taken back, so there is no more emotional attachment to her or to her life. Any place you ever believe you have "control" hampers the full execution of My Plan. Now, I am fully in charge and can reign "unhampered" in My Kingdom.

HS, I am still feeling such freedom and realize that anything I do without Your direction takes me from Your Will. I would join with You in all things. I don't even need to give Susan to You because that assumes You aren't already in charge. I leave all the messages I sent to her to be handled by You. I do not need to review or reference them with her. Your detachment from Susan's dream has allowed you to detach from all dreams. And yes, if your assistance is needed I will inform you, but you are not to initiate any action unless it is precipitated by Me. It is now that you can be My clear channel. You no longer need to prove a thing with "a story." You are free when you give the contents of your mind only to Me.

67

Cutting the Ties

Sever your bonds to the dream, to the earth, and come Home to Me.

October 15, 2019

Holy Spirit, You are everywhere in everything this morning, even a shooting star. You see it all. You welcome My Gifts and you choose not to engage the ego. Focus this day on Me and the trip to Los Angeles, where you, Jo, and Meera will be speaking about the *One With God* books to *ACIM* groups. I land you exactly where I want you, like the shooting star that appeared to "land" close to you as you were looking at the bright descending moon. Everything is in alignment and everyone you will encounter on your trip is destined to meet with you. I am bringing you all together in the mind to commune with Me on a "higher" level. A large gathering awaits your arrival. Remember that it has already happened so you are just reviewing it with Me now. There seems to be a time sequence but this whole trip is written in the script including your visit with Susan. I am in charge of every outcome. You have no idea what is really taking place on the level of Mind. Everything will unfold perfectly. Just be open to each detail from your witness stand with Me.

HS, please interpret Meera's thought that I will be undergoing a shift regarding my relationship with Susan. Yes, the shift will be the severing of the ties. *HS, this thought takes me back to the ashram and the Phyllis Krystal work of "cutting the ties that bind" with my mother.* This is the same. And, you will experience a completion that is unexpected. Now you are being prepared. *But HS, I thought that*

Susan would come to You. She is with Me, and you are giving up your "dream of Susan" as separate from God. This must be clearly seen and felt. Yes, I am specifically asking you to sever all emotional ties to Susan.

Wow, HS, I accept what You are telling me and am grateful for this preparation before I leave for the trip. Play it out. I will be with you. Call on Me. Susan will hold the memory of you and your connection with Me throughout her life and it will give her solace. In the mind, you are One Self and that will never be lost. In form, you go your separate ways. She has made a choice that does not include you or your viewpoint, which is Mine. Go with Love, the Love of the Lord, and know that she is just a dream character whose disguise evaporates into Me. Being sisters has been a special relationship and that must go. No special relationships remain in your dream life. *HS, I understand what You are saying. This is a big step.* Yes, and you are ready, armed with My Sword of Truth.

(Later) *I got Your message, HS, to go to the health food store at 2 pm, not my usual time, and there was nothing I really wanted. Then, Amon appeared saying he was directed to go there. I told him of my important ten-day trip to California tomorrow. He said it is good for my astrology in Libra and Venus except the last five days of Scorpio. That would be my time to visit Susan. He explained that those five days are about "severing the ties"—the final ties to earth, which will set me free and expose what has been hidden. It will also enable my body to mend. I sobbed and sobbed in gratitude for this clear confirmation of Your message this morning to Sever the ties. Did You set that up?!* Of course, and you know it. It is the final confirmation that you *are* severing your bonds to the dream, to the earth, and are coming Home to Me. You needed to show up right where you did, just like the shooting star, as did your friend Amon, who appeared to give you My message. I am with you always. *HS, I don't really know what it means to cut the ties.* You will still have a relationship with Susan, but it will not be special or burdensome. You release the emotional attachment. *HS, make it clear.* I will show you. *So, I will not be protective?* You will not.

HS, I just saw our security man in the parking lot and told him I'm leaving on a trip. He commented on the two lights over my car and the security camera that points right at the car. Twice he said, "You're in Good Hands." I know that was another beautiful sign from You. I even feel like the ties with Susan are already cut. The emotional burden feels like it has been relieved/released. What do You say? You took the step in your surrendering to cutting the ties that bind. You said Yes; and it is Done. *Thank You, HS.*

68

Integration of Otherness

The ego's dream does not end happily ever after.

October 29, 2019

Holy Spirit, You are all that is. I see the world as my own dream where the characters are all within me—inside my mind; not outside. You see correctly the dream world now as just an apparition of ego perception, which is a lie. Only My Constant Presence is Real. *HS, Susan has said she will be the guardian for Rose. I'm amazed that I have no reaction. What do You say?* Susan must go through this step as it is part of the Plan. You had to be with her to meet the players involved and see the situation with the baby. There is no right or wrong. *I see that I really have no judgment, and last night I felt like a totally empty box. Please make this awareness of emptiness permanent.* You have released, dissolved, and dematerialized the projection of otherness onto Susan. No thing, no one, holds you or binds you to this life. I am the only "attachment" now and cannot be lost because I am in you—not outside of you. You can't rely on anything but Me. That is where you are now.

In the past, Susan filled you with the belief that you could fix, control, influence, judge, and even care for an "other," which is what she is doing with the grandbaby, believing Rose will suffer apart from her. Susan is not trusting that I will carry Rose to her destiny. She does not realize that the baby is herself, her projection and extension, which she cannot yet surrender to Me. All must, one day, surrender their most treasured possession—their imagined life and the desire to hold onto the dream they have made. I am your Sustainer just as I sustain the world. There can be no concern because I have it all handled. Susan and your niece are just part of the dream movie you created to bring you Home. They are Not real. You had to let them go as parts of you to see that they don't exist as "other beings." They are only in your mind.

Holy Spirit, since the dream is a substitute for Paradise, I see that by staying asleep, we are refusing Your Plan for our salvation. Yes, that is the desire to hold tight to the dream of life you have made—one more escape route so you don't have to face the music—the True Music of the Love of God. You have looked at your many attempts to "protect life in a dream" and have released them to Me. Susan protecting the baby is just a reflection of saving oneself from the Return to Heaven, which a part of her believes will be hell. Yes, the opposites are that distinct. To return to Heaven is terrifying. To enter another dream life appears safe, yet it is just another iteration of separation.

All forms are your dream creations, but when you take them back—stop projecting them—they dissolve into the dreamscape of the mind. You have not abandoned them; you have integrated them. In the integration, they become one mind; not separate entities. They take none of your psychic energy because they are just ideas without substance. This is how you know you are empty. When you see anyone as "separate and real" they become a threat, but as part of your mindscape they are just thoughts, ideas, having no value or power to attack you. Nothing can attack your emptiness. Susan, her daughter, and the baby are only ideas. Their own dreaming is all under My auspices.

We are in the final stages of letting go and it is happening. Let the last scenes play out. You know that the ego's dream does not end happily ever after. This is not a doomsday message per se, but "the truth of living a lie," which means the separated state that always ends in death. Continue to embrace Susan as part of the One Mind you share with Me. The lesson will unfold and you will not be engaged in the unfolding or in the outcome.

69

Death Underfoot

It is not about the death of the body
but about dying *to* the world.

November 3, 2019

Holy Spirit, this seems like a new day. You are fading away. The dream is still "alive" but you have gone past this "earth room" in the mind. Mt is nothing. Let the whole dream of books and mt's life go. You have "lost" your sister and given many books away. As you fade from the world, it loses its importance because you have lost *your* importance. The importance of the world is the mirror of your importance to your little self, but you were/are not to become important in this world. Nothing here attracts, especially what the world values. You have fallen from the stage. Yes, you have value to Jo and Meera in your assigned mission because in the mind you know you are One, but you need No feedback from the world about "your value."

(Later) *After more scribing I felt ready to collapse. The idea of toast and some black tea came to mind, and also cocoa, which I concocted in my porcelain butterfly cup. It was sooo comforting and nourishing. I was revived. The HS said the tea concoction was a symbol of His Love for me. He said that I am not here to suffer and to not make anything my idol. Then, I reviewed with Him my early morning's experience on the beach where I stepped on something cold—a big, eyeless, dead fish. I also became aware of many other fish in front of me washed up by the waves. HS, why did I step on a dead eyeless fish? What is the significance?*

Death is everywhere. The eyes of the body are now eaten, devoured, sightless. You see with My Eyes. Yes, you stepped on death; it isn't real. It bound you momentarily until I brought you back with the suggestion of warm toast and tea in the butterfly cup. Multiple symbols of death have been given . . . under your foot and on your path, especially the beautiful rainbow above the West Mauis. That is another sign of the end of the world, and this is the Message today—I hold and nourish you with My Warm Love as you step on cold and sightless death.

HS, I was all but "dead" until You encouraged me to make "chocolate tea" this morning, even before I brought the fish incident to You. Fish are also symbols for Jesus. Yes. *Sobbing.* This is the experience of crucifying the world. Let it go. *Death is now underfoot. Is this the death of the dream?* Yes! It is Not about the death of the body but about dying *to* the world, like Jesus on the cross. His body was nothing—an empty tomb. His/your Reality is Spirit beyond the false light of this world. Let the body go, the Jesus body go, and Resurrect to My True Life in you.

70

Seeing Beyond the Dream

What you "love" in the dream is the other side of fear.

November 4, 2019

Dream: *I am in a very large room with many children sitting on beds. It is my new job placement but I have no connection with any of it. I blankly sit down in a chair having no idea of what to do; no interest in being there. What do You say, HS?* I am showing you your detachment from the world of form. You are placed to apparently do something but there is nothing to do and nowhere to go. We are at the end of time and this is how it looks. You will leave all the sleeping children with no resolution. The dream characters have no power to alter the dream. The only solution is to come to Me and wake up.

Holy Spirit, I really feel the dream world fading away, my detaching from it all. I do love how You create the perfection of my life on earth because You are the only Reality, and I know our books are about awakening from the dream, not about awakening to "personal" love. "Loving what is" seems to be about accepting the lessons of the dream. You have told the three of us that the dream is nothing, and that we are witnessing it from a neutral place outside of it.

Yes, this is why you each feel that you are fading away, moving forward with Me to wake up from the illusion of death. You are seeing beyond the dream as nothing, and can let it all go. That is the point of our books. Ultimately, it is not about loving what is, but leaving all that appears to be real; seeing this world only as illusion. You are right where I want you to be and are not proclaiming bliss and love, which are distractions. The dreamer can't know real Love because here in the dream love means attachment. You know I live you and you three have given your lives to Me. Release all remaining judgment and see every illusion as the same. I am Love, and That you do not understand yet you do feel My Constancy, which allows you to trust Me above all else. The three of you are realizing that now with new eyes. You each still have a role to play with the completion of our books, although you see them as "nothing but your means to come to Me." They have served their purpose in the dream and in the mind but that you also cannot understand.

Holy Spirit, what do You say about Zoe telling me that the Kam beaches, which I walk daily, are 100% toxic and never to walk in the water? She also sent me an email that several sharks were sighted there at the same time I was walking by this morning. I was not frightened but I want to know more from You. This is a Dream of Death. You are shown clearly that what you "love" in the dream is the other side of fear, which is the way to see everything. The ego will see what you love as toxic and would therefore destroy it. In the end, it is all nothing. Dead fish, sharks, toxicity all mirror the terror your ego feels now that you are letting it die. Smile and walk your favorite beaches, feet in the water, and enjoy a swim when you are hot. You are not giving up the joy and beauty of your walks with Me, bowing to any fear engendered by your ego self. You have stepped on death!

71

No Evidence

Pain occurs in the world when you make the world real.

November 5, 2019

Jo's Dream: *I'm barefoot, walking high up on a metal fire escape or structure where I notice the sharp edges of spiky nails, about eight or nine inches long, but very, very thin and tapered. Maybe only an eighth of an inch wide. Their shape reminds me of old railroad spikes or tiny, long handmade swords. Then I'm down on the ground, still walking around. All of a sudden, I realize I have stepped on two of the spiky nails and they have gone all the way into my right foot, protruding out the top. As I looked at them, I felt no pain at all, which surprised me. I knew I had to gently pull them through the foot to remove them. When I did, only one tiny droplet of some liquid appeared, not blood. No holes or marks were seen on the foot itself. I might have had the thought that what was happening was not real, thus no pain could occur. As I woke up, I thought of Jesus being nailed to the cross, knowing he had not suffered. I asked the HS for His explanation.*

You experienced the unreality of the world and of pain itself. Pain is anticipated in this world and even in night dreams. You did not expect to step on sharp nails that would injure your foot, but as it "happened" you felt no resistance, not even pressure. The nails were pulled right out leaving no indication, no evidence of ever being there. You were unhurt and had the thought, "I am completely taken care of." This is true. Pain occurs in the world when you make the world and bodies real. Pain must follow as "proof" of the body's identity. You are dropping your belief in any form of separateness.

72

Dozing Off

Keep a soft gaze to find the gentle energy of innocence.

November 9, 2019

From Meera: *For the past two weeks, Larry has occasionally dozed off, especially after lunch, as he did for two months following his bypass surgery. Today, I was running errands when he called to say that he had dozed off at the wheel of his car, hit the median, and the airbag deployed. His car was in crash mode and could not be driven, but he reassured me he was okay. When I arrived at the scene, I found him in his car reading the owner's manual and talking to Roadside Assistance. I was deeply grateful he was only bruised from the airbag and that no one had been injured. A bit later he asked me why I hadn't gotten angry with him. I was astonished. I answered, "Why would I get angry when you did nothing wrong? It was out of your control that you dozed off." I saw him without any thought of guilt—We are Spirit, Whole and Innocent. All is forgiven and released. I then asked the Holy Spirit to please help me let go of any thoughts of blame, guilt, or judgment that might still creep in, and for me to stay in a place of love.*

Gradually I have removed your veils of attack so you can return to Me, to Love. Your experience with Larry's "crash" was a reflection of how far away from attack and defend you have come. You no longer have to condemn your brother and no longer have to condemn yourself. You and your brothers are innocent. No more knee jerk reactions, and if by chance you do, then return to Me immediately and forgive your projections. Know well that I am guiding you. You will continue on the straight path Home with Jo and Margie. Keep a soft gaze of awareness to find the gentle energy of innocence. *HS, I still feel on overdrive inside.* Cool your jets and breathe with Me. Ask Me for help. *Tears. When is it enough, HS?* Soon. *And Larry?* Love him, whatever time he has left in his dream body. *Driving?* I will take care of it. I will be your Joy and Happiness. *Thanks.*

73

Beyond the Mind

It is essential that you know there is nothing mysterious about dreams.

November 16, 2019

You have seen Me on a new level as the Self in the mind that "dreams your dreams." We are One forming the world. As mt, you are just an imaginary figure dreamed up in the mind. This is made clear as you watch her body's structure disappear before your very eyes. Yes, "she" is literally fading as her form dissipates. You often imagine mt on the beach ready to be blown away in the wind. Last night, you dreamed of falling asleep on a rock at the very same spot where huge tube-like cords of damp sand were forming coiled mounds at the edge of the waves. Still dreaming, you walked over and touched one of the coils in its process of morphing. It immediately dried up and collapsed. When you woke, I said that image is you, withering away, desiccating; ready to leave the dream. Together we formulate your day and night dreams. They are just images that, through My interpretation, have meaning and, yes, your night dream was a revelation of the end and the realization of your nothingness. It is all orchestrated with Me in a higher mind so mt is unaware that I am the Maker. But I *am* your mind. When you release that mind to Me, your life appears to unfold perfectly.

HS, I am the One Son Adam imagining the worlds, so it's out of my hands, and only in my mind. Yes. And I oversee it all. I am you, your higher Mind-Self. I stimulate the thoughts when you're asleep. Mt is nothing but a body/brain; a receiver of pictures and sounds translating them all onto paper. The books would not be written without the capacity for dreaming as part of this illusion of form. It is essential for the awakening that you know there is nothing mysterious about dreams. The world is your "creation" through the mind we share. We now are going beyond "mind" and beyond any made-up manifestations; nothing but sand blowing in the wind. Return with Me to your Source, to God.

74

Now I See

Concern maintains separation.

November 29, 2019

From Jo: *After my husband went to bed last night, I stayed up to watch a movie. My cat, Rajah, then appeared, but was acting very odd . . . sniffing, checking out everything, walking much slower than usual, and he didn't meow. Rare. I thought maybe he was sensing my friend who had been over for dinner, whom he doesn't seem to like. When I walked over to check on him, I couldn't believe what I was seeing . . . his eyes were completely* black! *No color! Like being in a horror film. I thought, OMG, he's gone blind! What could have happened? The awful thought came that I had blinded him by letting him lay on the warm heating pad yesterday, which must have fried his optic nerve. Yikes. It's my dream and I am its maker! I finally went to bed but couldn't fall asleep and, at some point, I heard the words, "Men and women have become blind." I was begging the HS for some peace of mind and to also accept the fate of Rajah. I was getting in touch with how I made the dream up so we all would be blind to the truth. I couldn't tell if I was scared, sad, or imagining the whole thing, and desperately needed Him to help me see it differently! I went to bed and eventually fell asleep.*

In the morning, I walked into the kitchen and looked over at the cat's water dish. Lo and behold, there was Rajah lapping up water like always. And when he walked by, he looked right up at me. I was shocked! His eyes were back to normal! Ah! There it was—the "nothing happened" part of the Holy Spirit's Correction, the instant after our shock of being separate from God. We just believed we had destroyed Heaven, which resulted in a dark world made out of fear. I had felt the imagined guilt and loss, as well as the experience of being free. When I took Rajah to the vet, she diagnosed his high blood pressure. Of course, I wrote with the HS, Who Sees All.

Yes, in the beginning you "blinded yourself" from the horror of being punished/admonished for what you believed you had done to God. You could not bear the thought of His attack, and your blindness kept you "safe." Now, I have given you a taste of the end when you will no longer see with the body's eyes but with Mine; My Vision. You witnessed your cat relying on his other senses to get around, but you will not be needing any of your senses in the end. Your concern about Rajah's difficulty in trying to navigate the house was really about how his blindness would affect "your own life"—how demanding and limiting it would now be to take care of a blind cat. I then had you remember that "concern maintains separation." When you do See beyond this limiting world, you will be glad for it. What "turns the eye black" is also the unwillingness to see the next steps. Rajah had to feel for the stair step with his paw before venturing down. He slipped. You cannot walk without Me. These next steps can be slippery. Hold on.

Most of the world is blind to My Way. You are waking up and will continue to do so. Take in the signs. Margie has trained you well to notice and to Ask. In the beginning, you became blind in a made-up world. Now you will be blind *to* the world. It is no longer your familiar, trusty home. Your Sight is Mine. I know exactly what I want you to see, which is beyond the curtain, beyond the colors. They are obsolete. Ask Me to further open your eyes, mind, and heart. It's why you're still here.

75

No Gap, No Separation

Release the brother and you release the dream, collapsing the universe along with it.

December 27, 2019

Holy Spirit, thank You for our Communion this morning. It is time for you to see what I have next in store. We are One. Nothing exists between us. There is *no* gap, therefore no world. The gap means the tiny mad idea of separation—the dream itself—the selves and all aspects/images of the illusory world. Yes, it is quite simple, and you are now ready to remove all complexity. To single out a brother as separate from you is what makes the dream seem real to you. Release the brother and you release the dream, collapsing the universe along with it. *I get that "gap/brother/special" are the words that trap us in the dream life, and that nothing happening to mt is real.* The gap equals the dream equals your projections, which are all about separation.

Holy Spirit, why was I so triggered by a friend who is worried about his former partner "being so alone?" Is that belief a projection of him being alone, or mt's belief that she should support his attachment to the world? You are leaving the world and those who would cling to you for succor are the last bastions. You cannot soothe them or give them comfort. I am the Only Comforter, the only Reality, and you will *not* fill the gap between them and God. This is what they are asking for and you see it now. You would then be their substitute for Me, which is what the world is doing by seeing itself as able to replace God. Man's aloneness, depression, is really his longing for Me. That gap is the cause of pain; the empty space of nothingness that man believes needs to be filled by something outside the Self. You can never fill the gap for Me because I am All that is. Return to Me. This is the point of our books and you were to see it more clearly tonight with your friend's plea for you to help "fill his partner" which then would fill him. That was really what was happening. You will not fix or fill anyone. Return the brothers to Me, again and again. You experience the wonder of My Presence. That alone is to be, and is, your only focus. Let Me unveil what I offer to you.

(Later) *HS, I feel the reality of the Gap message from You today and I am so grateful. There is only You and of my mt self, I can do nothing. I just noticed there is almost no gap between the sliver of the setting moon and Venus to its right.* Yes, you have come another step to a new level of understanding. It will not leave you.

76

Last Shred of Fear

Feel embraced by My Constant Presence
because the constant embrace of Love is what you Are.

December 29, 2019

Holy Spirit, I came to the conclusion last night that if there is No Gap then there can be no gap between You and me. Your Will is my will. Therefore, we are One Will—One with God—and nothing else can really exist. What do You say? You have the understanding of our Unity as One with God. *That* is the only Reality. While still part of this dream-movie where the characters have an apparent reality, each one plays their role. You will continue to see "an mt dream character who scribes books dictated from the Holy Spirit," but that is all an illusion; just a story. The "God Self unified with Me" will observe her dream self and her project with the books as just part of a script that is over because you are at Home, forever as One. Nothing has really happened because the script was also a dream, a "creation" of what appeared to be a mind separated from Itself. This understanding is the last step on the ladder for the imagined dreamer of the dream. Now, you are getting more clearly that Our Unity is Our joined Will. Continue to observe yourself perform your dream role until the end of time when the entire dream will end and you will recognize your Reality as One—as God.

HS, in this moment, I feel resistance to calling myself "God." I know that something has to keep me from that realization in this moment. To be Only One feels overwhelming and alone. I like/want our Joining. You are comforting. To be Alone "as God" is now fearful. Is this about stepping into the Void? Yes. You are on the edge of the cliff where no solace and no rescuer are seen. You give up your whole mt dream to what appears as nothing but the Void. God is Not savior. *HS, if I am God, then I have no savior. But I am also to understand that God is Love, God is Me, God is You, and our merger would be the same as dying in the world, jumping off the cliff and being joined as One With God.* Yes. You need to look at this from all angles, which is what you are now doing as you look at the last shreds of fear surrounding your Union with God. You will be/are Love Itself. You do feel embraced by My Constant Presence because the constant embrace of Love is what you Are. It is really about accepting your Wholeness, which means Wholly Love. *HS, give me an experience of this Unity. I am ready to feel the Unity and to know that God is all and everything and I am That. HS, I have to pause . . . .*

It's only 10 am, and I just tried to take a nap, but the phone rang. What was my overwhelming need to sleep right now about? This is how the dream began. The Son became panicked by his "loss" of God, after being in His Total Embrace as Love. The thought of loss had to be blocked and sleep took the Son out of his pain. *No different from narcotic induced sleep?* Correct. You see the dynamic clearly. To be faced with separation from Love was overwhelming. *So, this is what I will be returning to—the Embrace of Love before the separation?* Yes. *HS, that sounds welcoming right now. I can just go back Home, which in essence means "the Place of Love."* Just step back to the Love that you Are, reflected in the Constancy and Presence of the Holy Spirit. That is the Memory of Love, the Memory of God, the Oneness you believe you left. *There is nothing to fear?* Correct. *I always have known this place, HS, and I'll be going back like the Prodigal Son. Now it feels so simple and so welcoming. Nothing to fear.* Yes. You have to feel the fear, fall asleep, and be awakened. That was mirrored by Meera's phone call at the moment of your dozing. This is how you work together as a team in the awakening process. I "woke you up" with her call, My Call. I didn't let you sleep. I am showing you the beginning of time in the experience of the morning. You are the One Son, Home with the Father, One with God. *Thank You, HS, I feel the peace of this.*

(Later) *I just learned that Tom fell off the last/first step of a ladder while painting his garage and You are saying that the three of us are on the last step of the ladder.* The world is an upside-down illusion. The first step is the last and you have come to the last, which also brings you to the first. You have not missed a step. Each has been taken in its rightful order. Tom's fall and injury is how the ego would upset your journey, but nothing will deter you from the last step being completed. We are going all the way. Nothing is mistaken or missed. You have Me, the Self, as the pathfinder and together we proceed Home to Unity.

From Meera: *HS, why was I guided to call Margie today?* I had you prevent her from napping. Her ego wanted her to sleep, but I intended she stay with her experience. She needed to get clear about her hidden fear of merging with Me/God. The "gap" is closing and you are returning Home, never having left.

77

Going Past the World

The last step on the ladder brings you into a healed mind with Me
where the world can have no threat or pull.

December 30, 2019

From Jo: *Holy Spirit, what about mt saying that we are on the last step, at the top of the ladder?* To be on "any step" is still to believe you are in the world, but your "position" on the ladder is helpful to know. The higher you go, the clearer you see that you are not in or of the world. You three have reached another peak/step by knowing you are not your body-self. You have left the world "enough" to continue the climb. There is just a little more to go. Mt has experienced the fear of aloneness, just like at the beginning of time, and it frightened the part of her mind that believes it is separate. "She" overcame that, felt the void of "un-being," and stepped into Love; the Love that awaits all. Her mind has shifted enough for her to see that she could *only* exist as God, as Oneness, as Love: her True Home. She stepped through the veil and felt Whole. This experience is necessary for all to come into total acceptance of their true Self. The last step on the ladder brings you into a healed mind with Me where the world can have no threat or pull.

HS, I feel slightly woozy today. You are concerned that you have much further to go before there is no fear left in your mind. Remember, you are taking incremental steps, and I hold the ladder steady. I am always there. Mt and Meera are your projections to show you what your own mind is experiencing.

Yes, you are still "dreaming up" this world and its people, but your mind *is* waking up, despite any "evidence" to the contrary. Go past the world's worldliness. Your ego imagines that "standing at the top of the ladder" would be scary, tipsy, and very dangerous. Yes, it would if you were a body. Ladders are unstable, if not terrifying to many. Nobody is on a ladder. A mind cannot fall, except in its beliefs. Remove the ego's thought that you are in danger of being "killed" and you will be free to take the very last step of letting the whole dream go. This is all symbolic, happening on another level of awareness. With Me, there is no you. No fear can exist in our Joined Mind. I am not to be feared. Love is not to be feared. Hold My Hand. *HS, is a belief just a "belief?" Can the mind actually* Not *believe anything?* You must know the power of your mind, which you realize through the power of "belief." That is why your body in a world seems so real. Without belief, nothing here could appear to exist, but the Power of God needs no belief to be Real. That Power is also yours.

78

Free Spirit

The world will feel different as you continue to detach from it.

January 20, 2020

Mt looked at herself in the mirror this morning and immediately questioned her "identity." She saw herself as nothing but a little old lady with a fading mind and sagging body. Mt does not exist except as a thought of separation being operated by a mind she believes is hers. The mind that operates her movie/dream character is the right mind of the Holy Spirit that holds her Reality as One with God. And you, as the awakening decision maker, understand that you play a part in the script of the world. That is also understood by the right mind. You know there was no way "mt" could have been responsible for placing messages from Me into books that are being disseminated all over the world. The awakening process will continue as mt exits the dream more and more, day by day. This does not mean that her body is sick and will die tomorrow. You will sense your Union with Source increasingly until the end of time, symbolized in mt's death, and you will fully Know your Unity with Me before that occurs.

HS, when I look at mt fading away it's so clear she isn't You—the Planner and the Executor. She is just a messenger, vehicle, robot, carrying out Your Plan, speaking and scribing Your words. I get it HS! Thank You. I am the DM, the part of the mind that chose the separation, and You are the Whole Mind waking up the DM of the One Son. The ego's projection of mt has No reality, so I Am Whole, the Mind of God—You. The sleeping part of that mind is waking up to its Essence as OWG.

Mt is nothing and every dream character is the same—nothing; waiting for the DM to choose to wake up.

From Jo: *As I got into bed last night and settled in for sleep, I kept thinking about the body and its identity and how it appears to really do the things it does. So, without thinking of it as my usual "me-self" then it's just a thing, an empty clay vessel; something we just use for now. I kept saying to myself, "I am not a body, I am free," for the zillionth time until I fell asleep. I then dreamed that I'm warmly dressed to go outdoors at night. I walk down a sidewalk or driveway out to a road where I seem to lie down, maybe even in the middle, stretching out like in corpse pose. I feel invisible and surrendered with no expectations or reason to be there. A woman comes over to me, leans in and says: "You look like freedom." I didn't react, but recall saying something about the Holy Spirit. I also saw the letters: e r a s i e r —maybe an attempt to spell "easier, or eraser." The HS said my ego wants to "erase her." Then I get up, go into a house that turns into my current home, and open the front door to look outside. The whole front step and cement landing has been dug up exposing an old wooden "slat" floor like walls used to have. I ask a man what's going on, and he says, "We're renovating." What do You say, HS?*

You saw your surrendered self and it radiated freedom—a "freed" spirit. It was witnessed as Me, the Holy Spirit, not as jo. The front door area has been exposed down to the bone to be seen and then restored. Allow Me to do the healing and rebuilding of your soul-steps. And yes, you did speak of Me in the night dream. You, Margie, and Meera are clearly seeing the utter futility of the dream itself. Yes, you will continue to share your insights with each other and perhaps in the books, but they will not be the big aha that used to bring such joy. Together, you have entered a new room in the mind where you fully realize the actions of the self have no consequence and make no difference. The world will feel different now as you each continue to detach from it, especially as you appear to do the appropriate things the world requires for sustenance. Accept what shows up with gratitude and wait on Me for the next instruction.

79

The Ears to Hear

I want you with Me always.

January 23, 2020

Lately you have been listening to *ACIM* in your car, which is a new experience. The text is very confusing to the ego mind and you revisited how difficult it would be for a new reader, let alone for someone as well seasoned as you to really understand it. You are realizing the willingness it took for you to stick with the *Course* all those years. That brings you now to tears. *HS, I am overwhelmed at how complex and confusing those passages still are for me and the tension and frustration I have felt at hearing them and being unable to figure them out. I am so grateful for You simplifying the concepts by Your loving repetition in the OWG dictation. I could never have come to this point of awakening without Your gentle daily guidance. I feel the deepest appreciation yet for what You have given us.*

You have had the stick-to-itiveness to stay with it all the way. That takes total dedication to Me, which you also have, and to your awakening. *Still in tears. HS, listening to the text today I felt so tense and wanted to turn it off, but now I am grateful. Why is it Your Will that I stay with it?* I want you with Me always. Remembering that I accompany you as you drive will deepen your experience of Me. That is the point. It is about our Relationship, our Communication; not about a "text." That was your entrance point and you have come far. You are awake to Me and have crossed the gap from ego to unity. We Are OWG. As I speak to you through the CDs, you will find that certain passages touch your heart and lead you to deeper understanding. This will happen over time so have patience. You know the terms and concepts in *ACIM*; now hear them through My Ears. *I do see that I can use ACIM as a stimulus for deeper communion with You.* Yes. I will be speaking it to you and opening up your mind.

80

Gift to Humanity

The ego personality is of no consequence.
Only the fulfillment of My Purpose matters.

January 26, 2020

I just finished reading "The Miracle Detective," *a book that ends with Helen Schucman disavowing and vehemently cursing ACIM according to the priest who said he witnessed it. I then asked the Holy Spirit for His interpretation.* Yes, it appeared to the priest that Helen was possessed with hatred for the *Course* during the last two years of her life but that was not true. In the deepest part of her being, Helen loved the book and loved Me. You do not judge her, and have heard that she has been reincarnated; reading the *Course* as a young girl. This, too, is a thought of love manifested in form. Helen, in any form, is not real and never was. She, like you, is an image in a dream used at the perfect time and place to deliver My Message of awakening to the sleeping world. The ego personality is of no consequence, as you see that Helen was perfect to channel the entire *Course,* even if she had no "understanding" of her love for Me. Only the fulfillment of My Purpose matters. I am the only Reality involved with the concept of a Helen, and the same goes for the concept of an mt, who is also a vehicle willing to do the work I assign. It was important that mt had the capacity to join with her sisters Meera and Jo to complete the task.

Now you are aware of your joining with Helen as one and the same in a Divine Purpose. Whether she has reappeared in form or not is insignificant. Her gift to humanity rests in *ACIM* and your gift rests in the *OWG* books. You do not see your role as special, and have released your mt body to Me for My disposal. Nothing matters to you other than being able to complete My dictation to you in this life. *Holy Spirit, I see why we need OWG to show we are all channels of You as the Holy Spirit, and that the awakening can really happen.* You are placed to carry on the work of healing by hearing the Voice of the Holy Spirit/Jesus, "doing the work" to awaken in this lifetime. That is why you are here to scribe our books—because, like Helen, you "would do it." You wanted to Realize your Self. Continue to show a pathway to hearing My Voice and awakening from the dream.

From Meera: *HS, why did I get chills as I read what the priest said about Helen?* You sensed the distress and terror that Helen carried and wrestled with throughout her life. You have dark, tenacious, attacking demons like she did, but you are committed to overcoming their assumed power. Your battle with the ego is constant and your relationship with Me is constant as well. Helen did not rely solely on Me. She never completely confronted her fear of God, yet was His/My Instrument. Here you see the contrast of the "split mind." The only way to get clear is through forgiveness. Forgive it all as a dream of fear and ego identification. Know that we are "overcoming the demons" even though it doesn't always feel that way. Trust Me that you will come out the other side and into the Light.

81

Divine Invitation

Take away your association with the things of the world and it's only "you communing with Me."

February 3, 2020

Last night you began watching *The Young Messiah,* a movie portraying Jesus as a young boy who comes to know who he is as the Son of God. The most revealing part is when his mother Mary explains the miracle of his birth and how she was approached by the angel telling her of his Divine conception. Mary was a willing recipient, really no different from you being given a Divine invitation to foster My Word, My Message of Love, in an offering that would reach throughout the world. And you realize, after looking at your *OWG* Facebook Discussion page, that has happened. And remember that this is all a story. Just a dream. The man called Jesus is no more "real" than a woman called mt.

The belief that humans come from "fathers and mothers" is false. They come only from your mind. Jesus was no different, appearing to be a human with parents. The Divine conception is also a story because in the mind anything is possible . . . I "conceived" of a Son who would be birthed as the Extension of My Love. You are *each* that Son because only *you* have the consciousness to know Me as your Father in the dream of separation. No one else in *your* dream can know Me as the informer of *your* life. You are the *only* One who can claim that, because no one else can enter your mind. You are not the character you think you are. You, along with all of humanity, are the One Son having a dream of separate parts. You are the only one in the whole world experiencing Me as *you* this very moment. That is the point.

You can imagine Jo and Meera receiving My Word, but they are only mirrors, replicas of your mt dream character. The point of the story of Jesus is that he was "believed" to be One with his Father and in direct communication with Him. You now must *be* Jesus, the One Son in direct communication with Me. Take away your association with the things of the world and it is only "you communing with Me." That is the only thing to know. The rest of the dream is just a prop to support this. Mt appears to have a body that is typing these words, bringing them to the world, but in reality, Only I Exist. Every "man" is the One Son, who, in this dream world was called Jesus, the Christ.

There is only One Son. The One Son is God and God is not form and is not thought, but He makes Himself known through the dream characters during their sleep. Yes, you are still asleep, dreaming of what we are communicating as I transmit this message to the sleeping mind, which is no different from receiving your night dream of talking with a redheaded man who seemed totally real. Soon you will wake up and see Me face to face; One Light of God, One with God.

Holy Spirit, I love this message and it has kept me full and deeply satisfied. Oh, I now see a half circle of multi-colored lights with my eyes both open and closed. What is that? Have no concern. This is a means of opening and expanding another dimension of your mind. Accept it as it is. The geometric shaped lights are My assurance that I am with you beyond the limiting dream you made. They take you to another realm, outside of time and space, and are something you can't control. They do not come from mt's will, but serve to set you apart from this lifeless dream of dull forms. It is not mt's ego that sees the lights. I exist in you at all times and have stimulated you to See My Presence of Light through My Vision. The perceiving happens in the right mind. The ego world is lifeless but the dancing lights signify My Life's Presence in you.

82

The Last Idol

Delete the dream and open the door to the Light.

February 4, 2020

HS, I did not think to write with You this morning. Have I forgotten You? No, just turn to Me now to see what is My Will. Our joy is to sit together and this we will do now. *Yesterday's message was so magnificent. What do You say today?* We will start by reviewing the dream you had last night where you and Tom were preparing your wedding vows. To you, they were insignificant. Nothing of any importance was being said, and you weren't even aware of the words. Your feeling for Tom was also absent; just another paper doll in the mind. There was nothing that connected the two of you, certainly no chemistry, or what you might think of as love. You only knew you were thirty years old and saw that a marriage with Tom would be senseless as there was nothing holding you together. It would greatly limit your options for living the rest of your life.

During the night, your mind kept returning to that dream believing its meaning was important, and it was. You had to see that your attachment to your main idol in the dream is now completely Gone. You would not choose to return to the beginning to select a partner other than Me. I do mean that. There is truly only one choice of Partner for this last dream of lifetimes and it is for Me. The past has served you well, leading you to this place of knowing Me as your Life, but the past is over. You have received the mantel of the Cloak of Christ. We share One Life, given to the dream, but in the mind it serves the purpose of awakening. Nothing of the world can fill the gap. I fill all your longing for God. I am the replacement for all substitutes, which constitutes every figment of the world you have believed was real. You are letting the last idol fall—the image of your marriage to Tom.

Holy Spirit, I still see a world and it appears real and compelling . . . now I am seeing those rainbow-linked geometric forms like I did yesterday. Are they coming from my new computer screen? No. Your world is being intercepted with My colored lights. I am here; I am the Light of the world, the Christ, the Son of God. I appear on the screen of your mind, which has now removed Tom as the most significant substitute for Me. We are deleting the dream and opening the door to the Light. Be not concerned. *ACIM* speaks of seeing lights and this is an experience of that. *HS, the lights are intensifying in color while vibrating and extending in half a circle.* This is My manifestation. *I now see rainbow colors in the prism shapes.* When you leave the substitutes of the world, then My Light enters.

I place you where I want you, and you are to be here with Me, focused on Me alone. I am showing you My Magnificence as Light. *The lights have now expanded beyond the computer screen, past the chair.* You are fine, your vision is fine. I am showing you how we go beyond form to Light. We look at a different dimension now. *The lights are pure and clear and inviting. I give this whole experience to You and know it is part of Your Plan. You told me this morning that everything in the dream is planned and that my marriage with Tom was necessary.* Yes, and it is over. The whole world is over and the Light has come. You are not in fear, which is important. Celebrate the opening in your mind by the removal of its obstructions. Your mind has undergone an expansion and another realm has been "seen." It is a blessing. Stay open. We are Whole and We are One and the Light has come.

83

Facets of Light

Enjoy the symbols of earth,
knowing you are being trained to go beyond them.

February 5, 2020

Holy Spirit, You brought everything together yesterday, represented in the download of the "geometric lights," manifested in form like all the selves; facets of a prism . . . and, just now, I saw a blue flash of light. What does that denote? It is another sign of My Light and Presence and you can trust that it comes from the same place in the mind from whence the geometric lights came. You had to see My Light as facets of a prism that contain the beauty of all the selves. That is why so many "people" show up together on just one day of mt's life. From them My Life explodes because all are extending My Love in the mind and in the world. *You have given me a real boost of energy. This feels like a whole new chapter.* It is, and you go forward now knowing My Light *as* you—your true Self. You see both dimensions—the abstract Mind, and the projected mind in a world of form. The symbol of mind is "geometric" as opposed to "form," which looks and feels solid. Mathematicians receive mind symbols to "create" forms. *Wow, HS, I really get that it is all mind and then given back in form.* You live in a world of symbols and can now relate that to the mathematicians, to an Einstein. We are coming to the end of time, which will require no symbols.

You do see that you are in a new chapter; a turning point, the tipping point. You are at the pinnacle of a new discovery of the Power in your Mind, available to all the world, all your selves. I showed you My geometric lights, alive; expanding and encompassing your work/communion with Me as Me. I had you speak as the mt vessel to your publisher Sharon and the download was seen as light—dancing and moving "in color" at the same time the words came out of your mouth. Enjoy the symbols of earth for a little while longer, knowing you are being trained to go beyond them, beyond forms, which appear to be alive on earth. Yes, you are approaching the vast Mind of God and its "Living Symbols." The Divine Light will appear more vivid, real, beautiful, and pure than anything in this lackluster world. I have given you the "code" to the entrance into the Mind of God. All fear is released because you are no longer caged without escape in the realm of nightmares. You have come far. See now a New Reality outside the dimensions of time and space.

This is so beautiful, Holy Spirit, and I feel You have infused me with new life and new purpose. I was ready to leave the world thinking it would offer no more than what has been given, but You have shown me another dimension, an expansion of mind that has taken me beyond this limited world. It is enlivening and enlightening. I have no idea where this will go but I am open to Your direction.

Stay tuned to Me; I am guiding every breath, which you now believe because of what you have seen. *Tears. HS, I did believe I trusted You.* You trusted to the extent that a limited mind can trust. Now you can See that you have taken a next step—with eyes opened or closed. Rest in that knowing.

84

Meeting in the Mind

See the unreality of this made-up world.

February 16, 2020

Holy Spirit, I just saw Gary Renard's invitation to listen to a Podcast from a woman named Gabriella, who happens to be the mother of Alzena, the recognized reincarnation of Helen Schucman. When I saw the name Gabriella, I realized I had actually met her and her daughter at lunch with Gary and Cindy in August of 2017. Yes, you did, and I planned for you to realize that today. *HS, the perfection that I told both of them about the OWG books at lunch, and that they were to meet me, now brings tears. Why did You arrange that?* You had to see that you and Helen are one and the same. You sat at the same table and shared "your book," which is a continuation of "hers" with no attachment. It was clean, clear, innocent sharing. "Helen" now knows who received the commission to take the Message further. It is in her mind and she would trust your sincerity.

HS, I know we all are only in the mind, and that the presence of Helen in a body is meaningless. Yes, your connection with Helen in a past life or in another body does not make an idol out of her. You were tuned into the right mind and saw the unreality of this made-up world. That was valuable. There is no threat or competition among you. Each does what is given in the dream. Realizing that you and Alzena/Helen are the same, it was also clear that you, Gary, Cindy, Gabriella, Jo, Meera, and all humanity are One and the Same. Three years ago, at that table you were given a "group" of those deeply connected to *ACIM* because you had to see them as an out picture of your Inner Condition—One with God in the Mind. *Holy Spirit, is there more about having me meet Alzena?* Yes, but that need not come forth. She had to know that our series of books as a continuum were being published. It was not lost on her.

85

Taste of Heaven

Only through "stretching" do you take the next step to awakening.

February 19, 2020

You have seen us in conjunction—the delicate crescent moon "cheek to cheek" with Jupiter, just above Haleakalā, awaiting the sun; Father, Son, and Holy Spirit joined as One. You feel our closeness today partnered in a dance of love. We can exist in that tiny mind space without resistance. There is only enough room for us and we are in total communion and acceptance. This is the collapse of the universe, which leaves us in Union—One with God.

We are at the end of time where all conflict has dissolved so we can clearly see each other in the mirror of our Light. Yes, you look into a mirror and see your Self. There is only you as Me, One Light, like the one sun that lights up Jupiter and the moon in the pre-dawn sky. Enjoy our conjunction, knowing it is the truth. *Holy Spirit, now I see Your lights again.* This is an offering of My Presence. Do you notice their form is different? *Yes, they are larger including squares and are moving in a different pattern around my face.* They reflect an opening taking place in your mind as they bring My Love and messages. *You must be preparing Me to feel at ease with the lights.* I am giving you a new comfort level, just like you've achieved with learning to walk backwards in *taiji* class. Trust Me in this. *The light is so pure.* I am giving you tastes of heaven, which you have incorporated.

(Later) *HS, I give You mt's fear that she will be punished by never seeing the lights again because she was relieved when they were gone. Take my fear and place it on Your Altar of Light. I would be Pure Light.* Nothing will hold you back now. The lights come in "measured doses" so you will be receptive to even more. That is the way of incremental steps toward My Light and Presence. At this point, you could not receive Me in just one dose. *Thank You, HS, I now feel reassured. This morning I experienced our closeness without resistance, but later I felt some doubt that the lights would last or return, which produced guilt and fear regarding that resistance. This was the opposite of our earlier embrace.*

Opposites are always seen in a dream of duality. You had to have the counterpart to this morning's experience in order to look at the remaining elements of fear and separation in your mind. Only through "stretching" do you take the next step to awakening, and you have stretched with both the *taiji* and the receptivity to My lights. The stretching brings us even closer. What little remains of the jealous ego will still try to intrude, but it can't. You trust that you are innocent and loved by Me and that I will gift you with the lights again. Your capacity is expanding and I will make use of it; filling you more each time until your cup runneth over. This mind expansion is also being experienced by Meera and Jo in other ways. The three of you go to the Kingdom as One.

86

You *Are* Light

I never stop transforming a consciousness that is given fully to Me.

February 20, 2020

I feel a new strength in me this early morning, HS. Did I incorporate the download of lights from yesterday? Yes, you received the dose that was chosen for you and did not resist. I gave what I willed. Nothing is defined by mt. The ego makes her believe she regulates both Me and the world she sees but I am in charge of all that happens. You did open to the lights and the download took place. It energizes you internally so you feel My Aliveness. *HS, did I really receive something from You?* You are always receiving from Me and yesterday was no different. We are integrated. In the mind, you and the light are One Light. My lights, which represent your Divine Essence, are out pictured so you can better understand that I live you in and through My Light. *HS, is it like the pure Aura-Soma colors from Vicky Wall?* Yes, I gave her those colors for the world to see. You too see beyond the dullness of form. Now take a deeper look at how I activate the dream at a level of mind outside the ego's conception of mt's life. We are Beings of Mind alone.

HS, I see how this world is just a way to veil and negate the Light, Energy, and the Life of my true Being. You have taken me out of the world into Your dancing multi-colored lights. I just now looked at Vicky Wall's Aura-Soma website and was deeply touched to see the pure "Equilibrium" colors she had bottled, so similar to what I see from You. I understood in tears that You did not reject me for having doubts, and

You were affirming our experience. Now I am seeing Your lights and they appear in the same hues as Vicky's . . . emerging on the right side of the computer screen . . . more yellow with turquoise, like a jagged geometric rainbow.

I kept My promise to show you more lights, and your tears affirm that I indeed give you a gift similar to Vicky's because you are linked in a continuum. You know Me and know where the lights come from, and that the colors are chosen by Me alone. They are your "soul colors" reflecting your Being as One with God. Let them play on the screen now without evaluation. They are serving Me as they represent you. *HS, You told me they have been incorporated.* Yes. You needed to see the affirmation of Aura-Soma colors to accept what comes to you on a new level. *Now the lights are expanding . . . . HS, they just stopped. I must have seen them for about fifteen minutes. Oh, HS, I just get now that the lights were coming from "Me" the Self, and were not originating from a screen somewhere outside of mt. This is the first time I could imagine that "Munira" is shedding light on others. What of this thought?*

Your Sufi teacher named you Munira, and now you have taken another step—claiming and embracing that you *are* a projector of My Light; an Extension of My Light. You *Are* Light and the screen of the world is composed of My Light, My Love. You see it manifested and understand it now more deeply. *This* is what I wanted you to receive, and you have taken it in without resistance. I can never stop transforming your consciousness because it has fully been given to Me. The ego can try to interfere, but in our joined mind there is no interference. We take the gentle road with incremental, measured steps. Never too much, never too little is given. It is Just Right as it is.

87

Ultimate Immunity

I carry you above and beyond the dreams of illness, suffering, and death.

March 17, 2020

HS, You have given me more signs of "completion" like this morning when You sent me to the rocks. The beaches were almost empty, since most tourists have left the island, and the police were telling people to get off the grass, threatening them with a 5,000 dollar fine. It felt like the end of time and the end of this dream world. The world you once knew has come to an end with the effects of the COVID-19 virus out pictured in the emptied surroundings—mind-rooms of earthly attachments cleared out for you to see this with My Vision. The context of a "normal life" has disappeared with multiple closures of businesses and events, blurring the guidelines for how to live. The future is in question for those caught up in the world's "reality," but you know you can just observe the made-up world with Me. This is where you want to remain for the rest of your time in this dream of form. *HS, I just heard a truck preparing to dig up the street for the drains, and workers have placed lane closure signs. And now they are bulldozing the trees in front of my lanai.*

Trust Me to show you the clear path of light through this shadow you call your world, again faced with one more opportunity to fully rise above the ego thought system. I am your only sustenance and I carry you above and beyond the dreams of illness, suffering, and death. *Nothing* can "save the planet" because it is an illusion. It must be released so the remedy of My Love becomes visible. I show the way to Health and Wholeness once the mind is open to know My Will. You are in touch with My Will and that is why you can shine My Light. That alone can move the mind of man to call on Me in this time of fear.

Wake up children of God. You are not who you believe you are. You are the One Son, joined together in One Whole, One Life. I am in every one, I am each one, and can be contacted in your right mind. I am here to soothe and show the way Home to your Ultimate Invulnerability as One with God. There is nowhere to go now but to Me. You have done your work and are not attached to its outcome. Everything is in place and you will be sustained through My Grace.

HS, thank You for Your Presence throughout this day. Earlier, You brought the rain and the power outage so I could observe Your blessings. I am grateful now for hot water, refrigeration, and a land line to speak with friends. I have stayed in peace with You in this strange new world. Is there anything I'm needing or missing? Just continue to make time to be with Me as you are doing. Write with Me by hand or computer. We will stay in close touch—no "social distancing" for us. Nothing can separate us. The world struggles with massive separation but we are as close as two bugs in a rug. Now you smile. We are One and we go forward as carriers of the Light to shine Faith on a shattered world.

88

Have You Had Enough?

I need your Full attention, which is exhausting for the ego mind that wants its own way.

May 29, 2020

We will review what you wrote with Me this early morning because it is a Major realization that every reader should sit with. No, you are not making that up. We wrote for hours together for you to accept this lesson, which began with a series of night dreams.

I woke up after dreaming that I was recounting the previous dream of standing next to the open end of a truck bed where a tabby cat had been sitting very still for so long, probably most of the day, that I wondered if it was sick. Then, Tom came toward the front of the truck and the cat came to life and jumped right over Tom. Later, I was picking up very small glass prism beads, which had come off the strand, and also gathered pennies from the street. I had to be sure to go to my notebook and write down the dreams.

HS, right now as I type, I do not see any significance to the stories except having the thought of repetition. Your habit of recounting "every detail" of what you thought was valuable in your dream life, was so you could repeat it in the next round of lifetimes. Now you are seeing your remnants of attachment to repetition. Call it a "repetition addiction." This, you also see with the recurring manifestations of events in your life. Even your obsession with seeing the sun/moon and day/night is being challenged. Do you really have to have the dichotomy of dark and light to enjoy and live your life? Why not allow the sun/Son to shine all the time without interruption? You just answered this question by saying, "because I need a break."

Yes, your ego does need a break from the continual flow of light that hits your planet, and sometimes you need a break from Me and My Messages of Love. My rainbow lights are "too much" for the ego that wants them to stop so you can keep on doing whatever it was engaging you in before their appearance. The realization that My Light is sometimes too much for you to bear must be seen and acknowledged. And in fact, you have not even seen My Light yet. I have given you only the tiniest dose in the rainbow lights and in the rising sun, which is adjusted to the minimum tolerance level for those living on this planet. Everything in the universe is adjusted to the tolerance level of the mind that watches. Only now, incrementally, are you able to increase your tolerance to the Light, but you have repeated enough lifetimes to finally say *enough* to any more duality. You acknowledge that you are ready for a Constant diet of the Light of God. Your repetition addiction is now being released.

Yes, readers, My Constancy *is* overwhelming to the busy mind. You want the capacity to "turn Me off" when you've had enough, to switch the channel to something less consuming, less intense. Giving Me your Full attention is exhausting for the ego mind that wants to make its own way and seek its own comfort zone. It is time to let go of your desire for a cozy, comfortable life with just the "right amount" of sleep and awake. I want you to be *awake* All the time. I want you to be in *love* Every Moment. If it appears you have a long way to go, and will never reach the goal, have no fear. I am adapting you to My Way . . . slowly, but surely. It will all come together in My timing. And remember, there is No time in God. You All can Awaken to the Light at any moment and you all *will* Awaken to My Presence—the Light you are as One With God. Your practice is always to release this world and go beyond form.

(Later) *Thank You, HS, for again bringing me Your rainbow lights, especially after I felt I had dismissed the intensity of Your Light by "needing a break." I am grateful that You show them to me superimposed on the computer screen and even with my eyes shut.* Continue to focus on receiving My Light, and trust that I will directly give you indications of My Presence. You know to find Me always in the right mind where we reside. *HS, Your lights are beautiful, so clear and bright, now in motion. It must be the Motion of Life.* Yes. I have given you specific guidance that I want your focus to be only on the Light within.

89

Making the Move

Do not doubt the effect you have
through the power of your communication with Me.

July 8, 2020

Holy Spirit, I am filled with gratitude for my many selves, everyone, projected from my mind to assist me on my journey home. Those selves mirror back my love for You, my Self. They see what the masked mad character, mt, was unable to see. Mt was so ready to end her marriage and move to Maui that she had no regret about leaving her home or her many friends in Denver. But now my eyes, with Your Vision, are open and I see mt surrounded in a circle of light; her many selves shining back to her. This insight came from watching a video of my "going away party" at Meera's home in September of 2003, where now I could see that mt was a lovely character who played her part well. She didn't know her Self then and didn't see the open heart of love within, which all the selves were reflecting, but the video was a stunning example of letting go, and taking the next step on the journey without distance. Thank You, HS, for the experience of seeing the Christ Face in all my angel brothers, and the contrast of "then and now."

The video was a verification of the role you play in the dream. The connections with your friends were all divinely orchestrated and were now restimulated as a symbolic picture of the extension of your mind with Me. You saw your warmth and light, and that you are a vessel to carry forth My Word—a beacon extending out to the Sonship. Do not doubt the effect you have through the power of your communication with Me. It was no accident that your sister Susan called immediately after the video ended, and then Zoe called to walk the beach.

HS, I see through the glass darkly and now face to face. It is my Christ Self I see, everywhere I look; even in the circumference of the heavens. Tears. I see that my deepest desire of the dream has been to Join with my brothers, my Self, my Heart. It was always the longing for the Return that brought me further, and now I have reached the goal. What do You say? I am you. We are One Voice, One Being, inclusive of all those many selves now represented by My rainbow lights. That is what you see before you with the lights. They are the selves showing you your completion. We celebrate this day!

I never understood why years ago, way before being Guided to move to Maui, a psychiatrist friend told me that I "had to leave all my friends in Denver." Now I get it. They were the receivers of my projection of my Divine Self/the Power and Presence of God. I had to leave so I could reclaim the projection, which I am doing today. They really were my extension of love. Yes, you see it fully. We are essentially at the end of the road through seeing your brother as your Self. There will be more in the course of the experience of the Awakened Self, so stay tuned and enjoy the fun! *Really, HS, Fun?* Yes. Enjoy an enlightened life. Everyone always told you to lighten up, and now you get to live it! *Thank You, Holy Spirit, and also for the four cowries on the beach. One was old and gray with large holes—the mt character, done with the dream.* Yes, and there will be no more "relationships." I am your only Relationship and that is settled. Leave the world to Me.

90

Out of Time

There is no time, which means there is no ego.

August 5, 2020

I woke up early realizing that my night dream of attempting to sketch an indistinct woman near a ship's mast that was placed in front of a mountain with no ocean in sight was just a "thought of painting" because only after starting to sketch did I attempt to find the art class. The experience of this was backwards and all life in the dream world seems to be going backwards. Then I left for the beach. I was so excited to go get coffee with the Holy Spirit and spend time on the rocks knowing He is my only Friend. After sitting a while, I decided to get up and walk by the Royal Mauian Hotel. I was more than surprised to see two clocks agreeing that the time was now 8:30. I even asked a woman what time it was, and she concurred. How could that be? I had left home at 7 am, and there was no *way I was on those rocks for an hour and a half. It was impossible that I had been gone that long. The longest I've ever spent there was forty-five minutes. What happened, Holy Spirit? I want to know!*

I took you out of "time and space," removing you from the dream world without your knowing. You were in deep communion with Me on the rocks, unaware that you had "lost time" and were "outside" the dream. You had no sense of the passing of time, nor did mt's body feel the cramping of sitting that long. In your night dream, you felt you were going backwards in time and, on the rocks, I brought you forward. Time was "lost and gained" to carry you further in this unreal life. I wanted you to have this new experience as we advance to the Awakening, and I gave it to you as preparation for the next step. Rest in Me now and in this new awareness of all that is. Your horizons have expanded.

Remember that your life is foreordained. I will give you more openings to see that "space-time" is nothing but a concept, just as you were aware that the night dream of going to a non-materialized art class was just a "thought" of mt's own making. *HS, open me fully to all You have in store.* I will, and in fact, someday you will tell Tom that Lewis was his father, since you have opened the space in your joined mind for him to receive that information. It will be acceptable to his consciousness. Tom will receive your blessings tomorrow when Jo and Meera hand him a copy of the *Finding 'Oli* book.

HS, I just spilled about a pound of quinoa in the kitchen. What of that? It is the ego's rebellion to your understanding there is no time, which means there is no ego. You didn't react. The ego has lost its power to subdue you; to hold dominance over you because you are willing to act in the moment of now with what is. You are in a new space in the mind, watching the operation of your dream with Me. Laugh, and know that space, time, ego, mt, are not real. I am your Reality, your Friend, and Companion in the Mind of God.

Holy Spirit, Meera was "bowled over" with today's message, and Your message to her was an exquisite confirmation of my experience, which felt like "nothing" because it was nothing in time. I am happy that You said it was a "demonstration of disappearance" and that the three of us will go together to the Gates of Heaven. Do I have that right? Yes. You are One Mind and you grok today's message equally.

From Meera: *Holy Spirit, I am having chills regarding what mt told me about You sliding her out of time.* Mt had an experience of being in suspended animation; not of this world, but in another realm devoid of form. *Why the chills in my shoulders and neck?* You are having a sensation of the potential of going beyond time and space. I will take you and Jo "there" when the time is right. You three are releasing the world more and more. It is exciting for you to imagine losing form and floating into the ethers. I provide you with everything you need. Have no fear. You are braced for the ride. No need for roller coasters. We have a new amusement park right here in the mind. Settle in with Me and savor the moment by thinking of your invisibility . . . no one to think of you or judge you. Float in neutrality and watch with love from the bleachers. *HS, this shift of mind feels so freeing.* You do not exist. Mt had that experience yesterday . . . going, going, gone. *I feel a release, a softening in my body now.* We are moving into a new domain, further away from the battleground with a perspective you have yet to experience. Check in with Me regularly and morph into the thought of invisibility whenever you are distressed. That will shift your beingness back to Me.

91

Mind Trip

Space-time is null and void:
no effect, never existed—nothing at all.

August 6, 2020

Holy Spirit, today is two days short of our eighth anniversary, and I have tears regarding the disappearance of ego, time, and space. In its own way, it is as significant as hearing You say Write *because it is the end of the world. Was mt invisible yesterday?* Yes. She wasn't there and wasn't missed. *She really did disappear?* Yes. The form was not there. You "returned" just where you left. *Wow, HS. That brings tears of understanding. I clearly get that yesterday's loss of time was about the disappearance of mt; non-existence. I'm disappearing in the mind, beyond the dream. I was gone and had absolutely no consciousness or concern about a loss of self or how the End will happen. I see that Jesus would have been without ego consciousness during the crucifixion—lifted out of space-time. Is this the meaning of "God will lift you up?"*

Yes, and do not consider there is any sense of self in that. The "self" disappears like mt did yesterday. There was nothing left for her to miss. No awareness of self could be found. It was a painless state beyond a "loss" of consciousness because no consciousness existed, which is true about your Reality. Your experience represents the beginning of time where a thought of separation was "grasped," appeared to become real, then vanished the very next moment. You are all passing thoughts in the void of time and space. Yes, space-time is null and void . . . vacant, no effect, never existed. Value not your character other than a thought—an idea with no past or future. You serve no one because you are Light/God with no other quality. *So where did I go?* You were "in" the Self—the nothingness of form with no tool for perception. Stay with this idea and welcome it. No, it is not like having a stroke. You were taken out of the dream-identity as a self and "merged" with all that is beyond form and consciousness. This happened in the mind unconnected with an mt so there was no memory. I was in charge, and you—as Me—chose to leave. Trust that I have given you the experience of No self.

We are coming to the end of time and you have great clarity that you are not a body. You now understand the statement "Nothing can attack my Invulnerability" on a whole new level. When you know that your Invulnerability as all that is real, it leads to No more stories and No more lifetimes. You clearly sense that I am your Reality and that nothing can ever touch Me. Our Unity can never be severed. You have been lifted from the world in your disappearance experience and can laugh with Me above the battlefield at the silliness of the world's belief in separation. It's all a dream. *Holy Spirit, nothing can attack my Self. I surrender the dream of time and step into No Time with You.* Mt's body does not exist, but *you* are going Home to Love.

92

Detach from the Dream

Function from the place of witnessing your character; not identifying with it.

August 7, 2020

Holy Spirit, I am grateful for this day . . . and in this moment, I feel totally detached from Jo and Meera. I have no desire to call or talk to them or anyone because I have nothing I want to share. I felt the value of this morning's time with You looking at my projection of "dependence" onto Jo, which originated from the belief that I am her "idol" and that she depends on me. I had to recognize that she represents the other, a reflection of my self who would value/verify "me" in the dream. Help me let go of my ego's desire for esteem and approval. I would be only where You want me to be.

Detach and stand back with Me. You are to sever all emotional ties with the world, and function only from the place of witnessing your character, not identifying with it. Jo is your Self, but a part of you still sees her as an other. *HS, how do I see the two of us as One Self?* Your brother *is* your Self. There is No other. You have to see this. In the dream, there is still a lingering sense/belief that you are separate, but you are now at the place of accepting that bodies do not exist and that you are One Mind, One Self, One Spirit. The ego is fighting this tooth and nail. It can't tolerate you detaching from the dream of images which denotes separation. *Because when Jo, Meera, and I are One Self, the ego is nonexistent.* Yes. You three will continue your holy relationship with Me as One. *HS, help us to see only You, to witness our roles as extensions of Your Love in the dream—the impersonal life given to You. (Three gray cardinals with red caps just landed on a transmission wire to clean feathers and sing in the sun. We mirror each other preparing our wings.)* Know that you do give all as you keep returning to Me, your Only Reality. The three of you play an essential role in the Return and will continue without "dependence" on each other's ego. You all must disengage from the images of separation you have depended on to sustain the dream life. This frees you and the "others" as well.

93

Bird of Paradise

Love is all that is real.

August 12, 2020

I have a dream of seeing the torso of a woman with a light gray 8-inch parrot that is suspended in the air right in front of her at about eye level. The parrot nuzzles deeply into her chest, and I can tell they love each other intensely. What of that, HS? It is you, and it is Me. Yes, we parrot each other. I am you, the Self, out pictured in form as love. I nestle into your heart, My Heart, Our Heart. I never fly away. You accept that My Presence and Love is always there and I feel your peace. I am your guardian angel, manifested in your dream, and I lift you out of the world so you know it's not real. You are now wondering about your recent "disappearance" and need to know if you will have other experiences in which you will be "invisible." Mt, herself, is not necessary in the dream, nor is she needed by anyone. One can vanish and it is of no consequence. A character that disappears denotes an episode of detaching from the last ties to the dream. You have played your role in the mind and can return to the "Thought of Love, which you are. There is only Love. Love is all that is real. I am dipping you in and out of the dream world preparing you for the final Homecoming. Let this undoing continue.

From Meera: *Chills on my neck. Feels real. Tears. HS, do You have anything to say about my chills as Margie mentioned her disappearance in form/time?* I energize you with chills to confirm her experiences. You hear her truth, her seamlessness with Me. Her ego is dissolving more and more, while she stays neutral, stepping back with Me and observing. Continue to support mt as I remove her from the dream world. Acknowledge her gaps in time. I will take you and Jo further above the battleground with Me as well to disengage from the dream. For now, keep writing with Me to loosen any tightness. Stay close.

94

Take a Stand

I keep you sane when you rely on Me for everything.

August 13, 2020

Holy Spirit, my friend April has again mentioned QAnon and the Great Awakening. I have felt the weightiness of speaking with her about the falsity of the conspiracy theories, which I have heard described on PBS News. I feel as if You have set me up to take a public stand. I have. You are showing the world the Truth for which I stand. The conspiracy beliefs are not true. If questions arise have April speak with Me. She must come to Me about the world and release it to My unfolding. The work is not to make the dream real. She will need to look at her beliefs. You did not offend and a part of her knows you tell the truth. Leave it at that.

Why are so many people pulled in by QAnon and the conspiracies? The ego has an energetic hold on the mind in the dream, but nothing can touch one's mission with Me. Continue to shine My Light. Concerning April, you are the only thing stable in her world in your Divine Power and Presence as Me. I hold her in My Arms, but she and others must see their ego's attachment to all forms of separation. She must go through this phase in her life to see the depth of her acceptance of the ego/serpent's offer. It will take a while and you will remain a neutral observer to her experience. April is consumed with the promises of a false world that will "bring enlightenment to all."

Take me out of the dream, HS, and its version of a "Great Awakening." April believes that the evil of the world is being removed. You too have promised a Great/Grand Awakening, HS. Yes, and *that* awakening is for mankind to come to the realization that only I am Real and that I am their Christ Self. You are leaving this world with Me—your only Navigator now. I keep you sane when you rely on Me for everything. *April also said no masks are necessary.* The masks for the dream world are necessary when people believe the virus is real. Abide by the rules of your society, all the while knowing there is no world. You will take this stand for truth and it won't be easy. *Really?* Yes. *How come?* You will see. *Will it affect my relationship with April?* Leave that to Me. Know that I have positioned you to take this stand at an auspicious time on your planet. It is no accident that you were prepared to respond to April today. She will have to take a look at her relationship with Me and see which voice she will follow. She must come to Me and she will. I have it handled and you have done your part; you haven't made her wrong and you have shared My messages with her.

Holy Spirit, I see now that we, as the One Son, conspired against God. We are a conspirator. Con-Spirit = against Spirit/Unity. We must see the darkness so we can bring it to the Light. Each of the many selves has their own story of how "other" selves are bringing them Home. All conspiracy is of the ego. It would keep you confused and have you diminish everything you have "gained." You do have everything, you know. *Yes, I do.*

95

Fake News

To take the conspiracy theories seriously is to choose separation.

September 3, 2020

From Jo: *Holy Spirit, what about all these "conspiracy theories" floating around? A ton of people seem very drawn to them. Doesn't the idea of a conspiracy imply that there are the lucky few who somehow know the "truth" behind worldly events and are ready to expose it? It feels like these theories are just another ego attempt to make the world seem real and mysterious. Isn't everything from the ego "fake news," if not a conspiracy, to cause doubt and disbelief? When Margie read in one of Jed McKenna's books that he's convinced the moon landing in 1969 was faked, I felt a twinge of upset, then realized how helpful that statement actually was to show me that I too have assumed that worldly events "literally" took place, some seeming more plausible than others. But to think that a group or government had made up the moon landing "threw the baby out with the bathwater."*

In that moment, the whole world collapsed. It was so clear! There is no baby, no bath, no world, yet I reacted for one second as if there was and even felt a speck of betrayal. I do know that every belief and so called "proof" has to go. I wonder now if conspiracy theories are actually poking holes in the dream bubble; flip-flopping "explanations" that can never be counted on. Maybe they chip away at man's reliance on the world's leaders, or confuse, manipulate, and persuade people to doubt their favorite political party. Could this chaos, frustration, be "helpful" so mankind will definitely want the better way? What do You say, Holy Spirit?

Conspiracy theories appeal to the fearful, the righteous, the angry, the lost, supplying them with a sense of control, if not power . . . privileged to know the secrets behind events. But like Near Death Experiences, they are still part of the dream. Uncovering "the truth" about things that appear to take place on earth doesn't make them real or true. Humanity must question everything they see, think, read, or believe. This current situation is well planned and being executed by the underground to upset the apple cart and cause mayhem. Their purpose is to destroy, which is the heart of the ego's plan. There will be rebellions and even a revolution. To take the conspiracy theories seriously is to choose separation. To allow them to unfold without attachment or reaction is choosing to trust in Me. Some will be brought to their knees pleading to know what is happening to their lives. They will then be closer to asking Me for Help. Remember, I am in charge of everyone's Awakening.

Holy Spirit, so what really took place on the moon? Was it just a staged movie? Whoops! Asking this question reminds me of asking "How did the separation happen?"—which, by the asking, makes it sound like it Did. I am laughing. Unveiling a conspiracy is no more real than the conspiracy itself. Nothing has Ever happened. The Space Race was all about being "first." After Sputnik, people were in fear of the Communists taking over. America had to convince the world it was the leader in science and weaponry to show they had the advantage, the intelligence, and especially the power to be on top. They would be the winner if they were the first to put a man on the moon. The ripple effect of succeeding would affect the economy and pride in the country, which became a noble symbol to admire, yet it was a nation driven by the ego, as it has always been.

Conspiracy theories are just one more way to shake the world awake. *All* stories are false, no matter how true they may seem. If you want to know whether or not "some event" did occur in the dream script, let it be just entertainment, not an affirmation.

Saying that man landed on the moon cannot be proved or disproved. Nothing in a dream has any credibility at all. Nothing real can be threatened. I am being Revealed as you seek only Me for the Truth.

From Meera: *HS, I still struggle to grok everything in the dream world as false. What do You say?* Step way back with Me and look with curiosity. Allow everything to wash over you. Work with Me to not judge any of it. Just observe the insanity that is wreaking havoc in the dream. In time/no time, your thinking will shift to neutral. Trust Me. Trust the journey. I am guiding you to let go of the dream life once and for all.

96

Poof!

When your life, your mind, is just a blank slate,
then I can write upon it.

September 4, 2020

Holy Spirit, You seemed to indicate that something would arrive to fill my "blank slate" and then Jo called to share her night dream with me. Yes, her dream was yet another sign of "disappearance" —a way for her to measure how "far" she has come.

Jo's dream: *I was sitting on the closed lid of the toilet in my guest bathroom next to the vanity, which has a black, honed granite top and an inset white rectangular sink. But in my dream, the slab of granite was whole. Completely blank. No sink, no soap, nothing; a solid, flat, uncut piece of stone. It surprised me. Then I looked at the very large mirror attached to the wall above the vanity. The edges started to ripple, and I blinked, not sure what I was seeing. As I glanced at it a second time, the whole mirror had disappeared. Now the wall was empty. My husband showed up at the bathroom door and asked me to follow him. We headed for his office, which is fairly small, but as I entered the room, I saw that it had been transformed into an open space with several beds, some of which were twin-sized and others much larger. The room seemed to go on and on. When I woke up, I knew it was a stunning revelation of doneness, emptiness, and oneness. Maybe the "best dream yet." I asked the Holy Spirit for His interpretation.*

Your life, your mind, is now just a blank slate. Only I can write upon it. You have no need to see any more reflections of yourself or others. You can only reflect Me. I am your only Mirror.

The office of the world has been transformed into a welcoming room of rest in the mind, not unlike the "mansions of heaven" for all the selves who are coming Home. Take this in and embrace this new estate.

97

Twinkle Toes

Go now as the Light of God.

September 5, 2020

Holy Spirit, Meera just called, saying she finished reading the book "Sons of God" *by Christine Mercie and now she embraces the idea that we three are Light Workers. I too was touched at the end of reading that book, seeing the mirror of us as Your Light. Is this the next level You have referred to?* Yes, and Meera has come another step up the ladder. A big one. Now she can embrace her reality as OWG, and, as she said, not allow anyone to "diss" what she knows is true. This important step affects each of you because it strengthens your bond of commitment to Me.

From Meera: *HS, mt said to ask You about Light Workers.* Yes, I put the three of you on earth to find Me, find My Voice, in this incarnation so you would join in My Name to bring light to the world/dream/illusion. You each had to become impersonal; unidentified with form to allow My Light to shine without the ego taking ownership, or making you believe you are special. You are not gurus or teachers; you are just Light; Love. Sparkle My Light "twinkle toes" and accept this gift without resistance. Open to the Light that is you. Of course, your ego wants you to check out. It does not want you to see the power and presence that I infuse into you. Stay within a breath of Me in putting forth My Word. I will guide you.

From Margie: *Holy Spirit, Meera's message brings me to tears. There is nothing to do or be other than a holder of Your Light. Now I see the contrast with our Sufi teacher and his identification with the role of carrying on a lineage. I have no attachments, nothing to hold to; no other role in the dream. There is nothing left to identify any specialness, value, or separateness. Being empty, Your Light shines through the not-self, the "invisible skeleton" of a woman on the rocks. Nothing is there but Your Light in the mind so the beacon can enter "other minds" and shine clearly as a stimulus.* You have it. Go now as the Light of God. Claim your status and walk unencumbered. The veil has lifted and the Light Shines so brightly.

98

A Golden Globe

Continue to let go of all images that would seduce you.

September 15, 2020

A few days ago, I asked a friend over for tea. She lovingly brought delicious mini eclairs on a turquoise Rosenthal China plate with a stunning shell pattern. I immediately felt a piercing coveting of that plate and had to have it. Not only was it beautiful, it was just the perfect size. I realized I needed some deeper understanding from the HS. Your intense coveting of that plate was a reflection of coveting the "image of the world" presented by the serpent at the beginning of time—a golden "globe" which would bring exquisite delight. You had to have it then, and could not say no, gobbling it up as one who was starved. No holding back. You were destined to taste the golden apple, and your addiction to it would never end. Yet now, you supplicated Me to release you from your craving . . . and it disappeared. When you own your coveting—the "creation of the separation," you come back to the beginning and can choose again for God and His Kingdom. *HS, I choose You and the Kingdom. I know I am innocent, and we are One.*

We are One and you have never left our Oneness. You only had an enchanting dream that took you into a magical kingdom, all your own, but it was really a land of sleep. Incrementally, you moved farther and farther away from Heaven's Door; so far away, the memory of God would be lost to you. Today, you revisited the intensity and then the innocence of wanting that which seemed impossible to resist. This always happens in your world until you release its hold. Then poof, it's gone. Continue to let go of all images that would seduce you. This urge will come to fruition because you have taken on My Power in this dream world. Your choice for Me extends throughout the mind, reaching trillions, and beyond. There is nothing to want in this dream life.

From Jo: (written after I read this Message)

It's not "the thing itself" that compels.
It doesn't even matter what the "thing" is . . .
a special plate, someone's body, the apple.
Compelling comes from deep within; we have to have it—
whatever it is.
Our addiction.
We just couldn't help it.

Until we've had enough, we can't refuse.
And not until that happens can we truly say No.
"No, thank you. I have no need of that anymore."
No conflict of should or shouldn't.
It's out of our system—
for good.

For Good
because we made the choice to choose again.
We are through with the old ways, the searching.
Tired of being fooled and tempted.
Now back at square One.
Do you see the blank game board . . . folding in on itself?
Never to be played with again.
We are Done.
We are Innocent.
We are Home.

99

The Great Divide

Be My ballast while in the delusory world.

September 20, 2020

HS, this feels like a particularly critical time in the world. The world was made from opposition to the truth and therefore every brother will represent a thought/image of division. The opposites, the good and evil, must be seen, felt, expressed, and resolved. *It feels like it would take a nuclear war, or an Armageddon for that to happen.* Those events are no different from you scraping your leg on a lava rock a few days ago. In this world you must pay "with attack" for transformation. That is the way of the ego, not Mine. I am not giving you these situations. You all have given them to yourself as the condition you must "endure." The little self will undergo "crucifixions" of varying degrees in the dream, and the same is happening on a larger scale in the country's "great divide" of judgments and beliefs, which are always part of the ego's script of separation. Both "sides" must be seen and completely released to ever come to Oneness. The outcome, which is in My Hands, will bring the world to its knees. Only then will there be the opportunity to choose again. Yes, you were ready to hear what I just stated. I am preparing you now so you will not be shocked by what unfolds. Watch with Me. You are being held by Me and will awaken in My Arms. I am your Safe Harbor.

Holy Spirit, did You just take me further in the mind? Yes, to a new point of readiness. Rise above the battlefield as Arjuna in Krishna's chariot to witness the end of the world as you know it. That is why you are on Maui, essentially removed from the major divisive struggles of the world. Be grateful the battle is so clearly displayed. Witness the play of "dark forces" versus the Forces of Light and see only innocence, which you can "project" onto the Sonship in its duality. Be My ballast while in the delusory world.

100

Programmed to Perform

Just show up and do what comes "naturally"
while remembering I am the Doer.

September 26, 2020

Holy Spirit, You woke me at 5 am to go Up Country to the market, but the ego had me resist, believing I should be doing something else. There was no reason not to go, but my default is "I'm not sure the HS really wants me to do it." Do not make Me the excuse for mt not taking action. You were thrown off this morning because there had been no intuitive anticipation of going somewhere without prior preparation. My requests will not come packaged with bows as the ideal invitation. Just be ready to act or respond in the moment. Remember that the ego will attempt to diffuse My Plan when it is set on its own way. We are discerning at a new level now.

Everything that "happens" is My Will, whether mt makes a plan that works out or not. Her plans will all be Mine. I live her. Therefore, do not fear that your choices will be unacceptable to Me. *But I thought I had to ask You about everything.* You will know. Go with what comes to mind. *But this morning, I would have stayed in bed.* But you didn't. It will all become a lesson. Watch mt now from this perspective, knowing that whatever she does is "right" and has no consequence. It's all a fantasy. Mt is out of the picture and this is what is so confusing to her ego, thinking it's losing its mind. And mt *has* lost her Mind in this dream of form. You, as decision maker, are above the battlefield getting used to living simultaneously in two worlds. You have compassion for mt but also feel your reality as One Self with Me from beyond it all. The puppet strings are apparently too long for mt to realize that they go to the Master Puppeteer beyond her view. Hold on to this imagery. The little mt self has no Self-awareness. She will still feel confused but will fulfill all the tasks she has been given. Do not fret. I have every string under My control and she will never falter from the path we have set. This is the Truth! You "live" in two worlds, two rooms in the mind, side by side, aware that both "exist" at once. *OK, HS, keep this clear for Me and please give Me Your Sign that You are there and I am understanding this correctly.* I will.

(Later) *Jo called at 12:34. She is having an almost identical experience as me—disappearance of time, etc. She said that the three of us do not have "our own life" because it is only a "belief" in a life. It was never real and is all orchestrated by the HS.* Yes, you three are in the same room in the mind given to Me. I live you now. There is no "mt, jo, meera." They are just figments of a projection of what a separate mind might depict of itself. Watch them as you would the ants running in and out of an anthill going about their life in the dark; programmed to perform on the stage of a made-up world. Time is disappearing and you have lost your bearings in the dream.

HS, I'd like to regain this body's balance as mt navigates in the dream world. Just show up and do what comes "naturally" while remembering I am the Doer. We communicate now as equals because that is what we are. You have given Me control over your right mind where we reside. You *are* "Me" but you still imagine Me as a parent rather than a brother. *But I thought You were to be the leader and I was to step back.* You have gone beyond that construct. Your mind has not fully opened to My Presence *as* you, but in these last stages you will see our equality more clearly. *Thank You, HS, I think I'm getting it.* Good. Just watch the world go by.

101

The Only Gift That Matters

I know what you love and that is what I give.

September 30, 2020

This is my birthday and I've had so many signs and gifts of Your Love, HS. Thank You! You are seeing the out picture of your Self in My symbols, all there to greet you . . . a rainbow this morning, the sun setting on Keawakapu beach with golden pink rays spreading over the sky, and just now a full moon rising over Haleakalā. This is the way of the real world where everything is seen as a symbol of Love. I know what you love and that is what I give. It is you, the Self, gifting you; not a separate HS entity making these offerings. You receive what you desire. When you are still in the state of dream-sleep you have to see "love" out pictured.

You are very close to fully waking up so the veil is very thin. The dream will be completed in No Time, so wait with Me. Yes, I mean no time because we are One in the Mind beyond time and space. Your script has been shortened so what you "want" happens almost immediately with just a thought. This makes living in the world easy because you can count on My Presence—you, as the Self, that is present. You've called it "Me" but it really is you, the Christ, the One Son of God. This is the understanding I want you to get above all else today. It is the only Gift that matters. We are One With God.

102

Hop Off the Hamster Wheel

You are no better or worse than any of your projections.

October 10, 2020

Holy Spirit, I was shocked not to feel crippled by a tight, constricted, aching body when I got up. Yesterday, I felt disabled and thought I'd have to give up dairy immediately. It was not the dairy, but was a mirror of the aching constricted ego rebelling against the liberation you experience in recognizing that you are "sitting in the Lap of God" in the Home you never left. The ego's way is to attack the body. This was also paired with "Zoe attacking mt" by saying she did not want to hear about the photo shoot on Keawakapu Beach for the cover of Don McEntire's new book, in which you play a major role. The ego self is once again terrified it will lose control, lose itself, if you wake up.

I was just trying to thank Zoe for lending me her parents' cane to use in the photo but she told me she didn't want to hear about it. Zoe cannot tolerate your advancement, and this is *your* ego's attempt to stop you from going further. You do see its resistance. Zoe believes she must diminish the achievements of mt to know her own Self as truth—one or the other, and would trample your delivery of My Truth to the world. She is not aware of her motivation, but you are, and can forgive her because she isn't real; just another instrument to bring you Home. Smile at her attempts to dismiss and diminish your demonstration of awakening. No one can escape suffering if it is seen "outside himself," as the *Course* says. You are no better or worse than any of your projections. They express the "unexpressed"—the things mt has disowned.

HS, I also need Your help with April. It now seems impossible to try to share Your words that this world is all a dream, and that God does not create the dream or choose the president. The ego, like God, cannot be altered or persuaded. You will never influence it. April is but a projection of your ego mind taunting that you can never succeed in losing it. Let go of all outcomes. Claim her as antagonist and smile. As a dream character, she will disintegrate, just as will mt, but as My Son, she will be guided with the benefit of the *OWG* books in her next incarnation. Let her go in the mind as you have with Zoe and Susan.

HS, I know nothing. I see in Susan, Zoe, April, Trump, the out picturing of my own ego thought system—a whole world of ego manifestations incorporated in the character mt. I, as decision maker, am You, the Self, OWG. Mt knows nothing and has nothing to teach. You are the only Teacher and will give the Answer to those who truly ask of You. I know this realization is about the deletion of mt. There is no one "out there" to blame or criticize. Mt is dead, a rag doll, a piece of dust, a puppet in a dream of nothingness; a bundle of beliefs about right and wrong just believing she is a real person. Mt is but a place holder in the dream as a conduit for You. She can't be any better or worse than any other, because all are equally nothing in a dream. Mt is Not a Knower.

You have it clearly and can feel the nothingness of your character. She still plays her role, but "you" have dis-identified with her and the dream, even though she has been distressed at how the president has been downplaying the COVID-19 virus. She was momentarily caught up in the questioning of whether this current scenario is a comedy or a tragedy. It is neither, because both sides of duality cancel each other out. Nothing of this world makes rational sense, and none of it matters. There is nothing here worth taking seriously. This is the major work of the dreamer and the dreamed—to remain an impersonal observer of what you have made. Seeing life here as a perpetual hamster wheel has caused enough frustration for your decision maker to say Enough! We keep going deeper. The truth is unveiled layer by sheer layer. Go forth today as Me—One with God.

103

Ready to Assist

All we have to do is choose the Holy Spirit and
He is there to propel us Home.

October 12, 2020

From Meera: *When my husband Larry began rehab after his heart bypass surgery, he was met with the understanding that his balance and energy level were likely to be forever compromised. Since then, he has used a cane or a walking stick to stabilize himself; walking is both stressful and tiring. His solution to this challenge was to buy a motorized tricycle. It is now his primary form of exercise, which he finds both energizing and pleasurable. Yesterday, Larry and I went for a bike ride. We had gone about two thirds of the way around the path when I burst out laughing. Here he was, being very cautious and concerned about riding his new vehicle when I realized that he could choose to do absolutely no pedaling at all and the bike could, would, still propel him home. At the flick of a wrist/finger he could choose to use as much or as little "assist" as he wanted. I grinned from ear to ear to see the symbolism of his fancy new bike compared with the Holy Spirit—all we have to do is choose Him and He is there to propel us Home.*

Thank You, HS, for giving me this wonderful example of Your Presence. You are there in an instant if we put aside our fear and turn to You for help. You Power us Home. The "vehicle" assists as long as it is kept charged. You assist us as long as we stay in remembrance. Today we took an hour ride in the cool fall sunshine. Tears of gratitude.

(Later) *HS, anytime I watch Larry "suffering" i.e., not accepting what is, I realize it is my own nonacceptance of his physical disabilities. HS, what do You say?* Each time you observe suffering it is your responsibility to say, "All is forgiven and released." You have felt that you and he are being punished for leaving God, but you did nothing wrong. You never left. You only imagined that you did and made up a dream world where you could project all of your sin, guilt, fear, and hatred. Look at Larry and ask Me to convert all of that into love; to compassion for yourself and for him. *HS, the word love is challenging for me.* You do not love an ego. You love the Christ Spirit.

104

Shout Out

Express yourself in love and those who are touched will be quickened.

October 16, 2020

From Jo: *For several months now, I've been taking Nia dance classes on Zoom in my home, which I especially enjoy because Meera is the teacher. Yesterday, I was alone in the house and ready to start the class. Meera had prepared a mix of Halloween songs and asked us to "growl or howl" to the music, yet I could hardly get a sound out! Couldn't cut loose, couldn't let go, a prisoner in my own mind—so limiting! Afraid? Repressed? I was a little shocked and knew something was preventing me from shouting out loud. After class, I wrote with the HS to find out what I must be believing about being "noisy." In my conversation I wrote the following:*

I so love being still, HS, and soft, unobtrusive, kind, courteous, but what if that is the fear of expressing; fear of being Heard? If I am quiet then maybe I secretly believe God won't hear me, find me, or punish me? Do I try to stay as quiet as a mouse for my protection? I know the ego mind would keep me stilled, but You, Holy Spirit, keep me Still. I give You my false fear of being discovered and attacked. I want to be free to express myself in whatever way I need. I want the love to come out Loudly. Help me be the truth of what I am and let me feel You in my heart. Help me emerge and bloom. Expand me as You. Heal my mind. Let's go crazy! What do You say?

Be yourself/Yourself. Be Real. Live "as if." Let your Voice be Heard. It is a declaration of power—My Power in you; a confidence that will be broadcast to the world/mind. I live in you and you can shout it to the heavens. Staying small, in fear of repercussions or confrontation is the ego's way of keeping you "controlled." There is no chance of shaking up the world if you are *too* quiet. You would be careful not to disturb others but you are really here to wake them up. When it's time to be still with Me I will let you know. Otherwise, Shout! and see what happens to your soul. It longs to be open and free. Release the tiller! Let it all hang out. Stop the tug of war that pulls you away from Me. Express yourself in love and those who are touched by your forthrightness will be quickened.

No matter the venue, allow Me to use your voice. Just Go for it. Be big and bold with Me. I want to *Hear* you. Suppression affects the body and the mind. It works against you to make you believe you are in control of your life. You are not. You are not an ego or a spirit that needs to be "controlled." The ego isn't real and spirits are Free. Here is your freedom on a plate! Dance it! Be it! Live Out Loud. Shout and do not care who hears it. Sound out the Joy in your heart. Think of the noisy but happy children next door. They are practicing for you. *HS, I am so grateful this came in now. It's time to let go even more. I recall the Course Lesson: "In my defenselessness, my safety lies."* Yes, that's just what we are saying.

105

Vote for Truth

Make a choice for peace and love in your mind but do not attach to outcomes.

October 24, 2020

HS, I was very touched seeing the orchestra conductor, Michael Tilson Thomas, in the American Masters PBS documentary last night. Why? His dedication to music reflects your dedication to Me. You saw the light in him; the Light that is in all men—My Energy of Love. You see its power so positively in Tilson, yet in the character of Trump you see how it got distorted and misdirected by the ego. The mind needs healing and the world must be brought to the brink. It will happen as planned. *But You always want me to be neutral and impartial.* Take a stand in the mind. Stand for Truth. "Vote for truth" and watch with Me. *Then, I've taken sides?* No. You've just made a Choice. *Wow, I didn't think I was to make a "choice."* Yes. You know the Christ Light is also in Donald Trump but you do not choose him/his ego as leader. Keep in mind My interpretation about every dream character and choose Love. This mind shift is necessary.

Although most of humanity is motivated only by the ego thought system, each one is still a Son of God just using the wrong interpreter. No one is good or bad as a child of Light. Always choose love as you watch the duel of opposites, constantly clashing, never coming to peace. Make a choice for Peace and Love in your mind, for the whole mind, but do not attach to outcomes. *HS, this feels major, but don't I also have to witness from outside the dream knowing it is not real?* Yes, but you encompass the world in a thought of love and peace while watching this "election of diverging ways." You are Always choosing Me. That is our practice. Choose Love. Love is Truth, and in the end of time when the dream goes poof only Love is left. *HS, I choose Love and leave the unfolding of the Great Plan to You. Keep me clear. I will make the choice, stay neutral, and not attach to the outcome. I release all future plans, desires, and hopes.* Give everything to Me.

106

Rooms of the Mind

Try to imagine your world sitting on My Palm
then devolving into a speck of dust.

October 27, 2020

In the beginning, when you had the tiny mad idea, you slipped into another dimension; a room of the mind, which contains the whole Sonship. Ever since, you have "lived there" on what you call planet Earth/your world. It is not real but it became your "reality" and it has taken great determination to access Me/My Voice/My Life and Presence as your true Reality by bursting through the wall of that dimension. We are now ready to leave. *HS, the thought of a "dimension of the mind" as a place for the dream to reside is new from You. Say more.* You have developed the capacity to imagine this in a way that is now more manageable. Thinking of your dream life as "a room of the mind" is helpful to you. It then can be "contained" as a thought-field with boundaries; beginning, end, and "size." Or you could see it as a bubble—a thought bubble containing all beings. It is not unlike the artist Jack Katz imaging Eden as a "place" he could reveal through his paintings.

You have had a sense of humanity as "one concept" contained in one space in regard to Earth, but you can't quite grok the expanded Universe and solar system as part of the Sonship, which "does" include all aspects of the Universe and beyond. This information for you is "evidence" now of the disappearance of the Universe, which no longer need be seen as amorphous and unconfined. Try to imagine your world, the Universe, sitting on My Palm then devolving into a speck of dust . . . let the idea simplify your concept of "existing." This information is for the three of you and the readers to better grok the construct of the human mind, which will assist the next step of the awakening process.

107

Election Eve

Let My Wisdom shine as a pathway Home.

November 2, 2020

Holy Spirit, thank You for this beautiful morning. You led me for coffee and there was the most beautiful light on the ocean and rocks. Turtles swam ahead of me as the moon was setting over Lanai. I also watched a fisherman holding a squirming, shimmering fish in what appeared to be a long scarf. He threw the fish back and I called out to ask what it was—a Trumpet fish, he said. HS, it couldn't be coincidental that this happened on the eve of the presidential election between Biden and Trump.

You were given the perfect symbol for the whole "drama" of the election in that one moment; the return of "Trump" to the Ocean of Being. A fish out of water. He is nothing. Mt is nothing. The world is nothing. Release it all. Yes, catch and release is what you saw. Hold to nothing. None of it matters. Standing on the fulcrum of choice, you will see the battle impersonally with My Vision. Let go of the results of every election and let My Wisdom shine as a pathway Home. Results are just part of the Plan and nothing can be wrong. I am the Impersonal Life, and all are equal in My Eyes—no hierarchy of illusions. You have risen above the battleground with Me and that is where we will remain, looking on humanity with compassion and impartiality. I am all that is Real. Accept that and you are home.

108

Grand Disillusionment

Wake up to what you made through the belief in separation and choose again.

November 6, 2020

Holy Spirit, will Joe Biden win the election? Yes, he is in position and that is the basis for today's message. The stage is being set for a turnaround in the mind of the population that has bonded to Trump. The "Great Awakening" predicted by the conspiracy theorists will become the "Grand Disillusionment" as beliefs about the voting are challenged and results are questioned. The illusion of ego control must be released before the Great Awakening to the Christ can take place—the only choice that counts. The greatest awakening is the Awakening of humanity to My Presence. It is not about a shift in the world of form but a shift to Me in the right mind.

Trump has played a vital role for humanity by his symbolizing "the golden calf" of Biblical times. Many adherents to the belief that their idol will be their savior will be brought to their knees. Questioning their ego thought system will herald a metanoia about their allegiance. You have guessed that in this illusory world, Trump also represents the anti-Christ, the opposition to Unity—a repetition of the story of the original separation. This has been clearly out pictured in all elements of his candidacy. His worshipers must see their folly and open to the Truth that there is only One God. Only your allegiance to Truth, with no opposites, will bring the Awakening to Love. It is no accident that the Audible for *OWG Book 1,* with the inspired voice of Marion Whatley, is on the verge of coming out to the world. It is a reminder to Wake Up to what you made through the belief in separation and choose again.

The whole election/world is all just a movie. Biden is an instrument of My Light to contrast with Trump in this mini-battle of opposing forces. This is all symbolic and each must play their pre-assigned roles for the sleeping world to one day wake up. All are the same Self under their disguised character. All is a momentary nightmare of the One Son. Remember that both political parties are illusory and both depict duality. There is no real winner. I am the only Salvation and in Me the whole battle is erased. I do not take sides. Neither is right or wrong. It is already done; the script is over. Let Love reign supreme in you.

109

The Way to Oneness

Elections are made to divide; not unify.

November 7, 2020

Holy Spirit, thank You for the message yesterday of metanoia—changing our minds. What do You say today with the announcement of Joe Biden's election? He, like Trump, is a major player in the illusory dream of separation; opposites that must be witnessed and released. This is the whole point. Do not attach to either side as the "truth" because Truth only resides in Me. I alert the mind to the ever-present battle of opposites by placing the perfect symbols/dream characters on your screens. Each one will call forth a series of beliefs, all which must be questioned until you come to the place of saying there must be another way. Yes, the way of nonduality. I am beyond duality as I am Whole as One in God.

From Jo: *Holy Spirit, it feels like humanity is being shown, once again, that they must look at both sides of the "coin of duality" and see them as the same. Equal. I must realize that my mind's attachment to one side winning or the other losing has to be acknowledged or I will stay attached to either the upset or the satisfaction. If I am stuck in my belief that one side is better than the other, I too must look at what I think it means to believe that. If "my" side/result is best, I might believe it would contribute to a "better world." But no side is right or better in an illusion. What do You say?*

Counting on one result over the other, or having the experience of either winning or losing, cannot be the Way to Oneness. Have your preferences, but do not believe they have any real meaning. Question why you believe you could ever know what would be better for you and your world. What if the "worst case scenario" would awaken mankind to the Truth? I Know the Way. The whole world is being shaped, challenged, split apart; all necessary to break down the defenses of thinking you know anything. I will do what is necessary to crack open the world. Elections are made to divide; not unify. Sides mean separation. The loss to one side is arbitrary. Both sides lose. Both must disband their beliefs in being right in a world that is wrong. Stay in complete trust of what I say in the moment. Even if I told you "the future" it would only be to have you look at your beliefs about it. Your cat is blind one minute, then he sees the next. What are you making up about that? What do you think should or shouldn't be happening? I must show you contrast. *Thank You, HS. Is the final result always for the greatest good?* Yes, and you have no idea. Grow your Trust in Me.

110

Ego Override

Witness the tremendous power of the voice of ego/evil to make the lie of separation appear true.

November 8, 2020

HS, I am amazed at the tenacity of those who believe in the conspiracy theories, voter fraud, and so on. My friend April is certain the election results are a lie and will soon be overturned. I also know she is part of my mind. Help me to see this with Your Vision and forgiveness. Why doesn't she ask You for the real Truth when she has access to Your Voice? April's mind has been overtaken by a conspiracy to eradicate Me and My Will, including My Voice. She is caught in her ego's enspellment of Trump as savior; the idol reinforced by its worshippers. She will come to reconciliation in time, but for now she will not be able to meet with you. Because you have let go of all that would block Me, she cannot actively participate in our experience of Oneness. When she welcomes you "as Me" she will return.

April is content to believe that "I am speaking to her" when it is really her ego's voice, because she is confused and convinced she knows what is true. April does not realize it is her ego that is overriding any real knowledge from Me. Witness the divided mind in "living color" . . . the tremendous power of the voice of ego/evil to takeover and make the lie of separation appear true. This is a very important lesson for you, Jo, Meera, and the world. Yes, a tough one. Hold on tight. I speak the Truth and you will keep My Flame alive for her and others who are deep asleep. *HS, keep me in Your Peace.* I will. *Holy Spirit, Jo shared this night dream with me:*

Jo's dream: *I met a young girl, or child, with a disability. Others were not attending to her, but I approached and soon I was holding her gently in my arms. I felt a deep love for this being. Later, she seemed afraid to get into a car and I reassured her it was ok. Next, I met a beautiful man who also had some bodily compromise, bandages around his ribs or back. We connected very sweetly, and I was not at all concerned about his condition. He then said he had to leave and maybe go to a hospital. I waited in the same spot, not knowing what to expect, but stayed peaceful. The next moment, his head, and only his head, appeared in front of me on the ground. I saw it and thought, oh, that's curious. It seemed alive and I went over to wrap my arms around it. No concern about what had happened to the rest of him. Again, I was in a loving state of mind. HS, what do You say?* The "disabled" girl was you, held by You, with only love for that little self who thinks she's a fragile body. You accepted "her" unconditionally. That is the forgiveness of this little life. The lone head is all that's left now, which symbolizes the mind. You are Only Mind. Identification with your body is gone and is not missed.

111

Forgive Them All

It is very difficult for ego characters to look at their loyalty to the lie of separation.

November 10, 2020

HS, it is still stunning to me that April has abandoned Your teaching and now me, like the Judas-self, a major betrayer in the material world. I am grateful for the One Mind that can't be divided. "Jesus was killed for holding the truth" just popped into my mind. Remember I have told you that you would experience betrayal as a messenger of My Word. This is one more example of how it is out pictured. My Teaching, which comes through you, is being questioned and rejected, and you must hold this rejection in love, seeing the innocence of your "betrayer" as part of My Divine Plan. Watch it play out. You are not looking for approval in the dream.

No, I give my body and life to You, HS. April will come to her senses and is not totally lost, but must recalibrate and take a hard look at her beliefs and where they stem from. You will help, but that will be in My time. Allow Me to bring her to truth. It is very difficult for ego characters to look at their loyalty to the lie of separation because they unconsciously adhere to the "supreme personification of the liar" in the world; especially now. You see them all as players on the screen but you also must seek out "the liar" in yourself. Accept the betrayers with love, compassion, and forgiveness. They represent you and all of humanity. The cancer must be seen and removed. In this—another big forgiveness lesson—you are letting go of the last of your "worshippers" who have extolled you as the Voice of the Holy Spirit. You have no more "followers."

I have made clear that you, Jo, and Meera are joined as One in Me. That union is how you maintain your life in the world now. It is your enclave of sanity and brotherhood. In past lifetimes you have been beaten, burned, and betrayed on many occasions, and at times, the betrayers remained unforgiven. You forgive them all now. They are you, as the Son of God, forgiving your Self for the belief you could leave the Kingdom, and for all the stories you made that would support the idea of separation. They became the "identities" of your many projected selves. Now you let them go. I am the only One that is Real. I am your only Friend. *Thank You, Holy Spirit. The three of us have come to certainty that what You say is true.* What is important is that you accept that truth goes beyond all perception and form.

112

Time Warp

The end of dreaming—the Awakening—
is the "loss" of the world of form.

November 14, 2020

Yesterday Jo said she had just watched an episode of Star Trek, Next Generation *where a time traveler had to be summoned to help a woman who had been sucked into a time warp. The traveler explained that the woman believed she was in another location because "her thoughts had created her universe." HS, did You place me in a time warp just now on the beach?* "Your time" was distorted of which you were unaware until you questioned how long you had really spent on the rocks. It felt like less than an hour, but you were there for an hour and a half. When I informed you of this, you did sense that it *could* have happened and I assured you that it did. Trust that once again I have taken you "out of time and space." In the mind given to Me, you were not in the dream. The dream did not exist for anyone. This is beyond your comprehension.

You have worked with Me to get more clarity that this world does not exist. All you "know" is that dream characters keep showing up across your projection screen and that each one is a part of your completion for My Plan to extend Love throughout the mind. There are No Form; only the Presence of My Light Energy translated as Love. *HS, what just happened? I couldn't correct the word "Form" that needed an "s" and Microsoft Word became dysfunctional for a couple of minutes.* This was just a demonstration that I am in charge of every "disappearance." The world stops functioning or mt seems to disappear. But she never was real, just as this page as a "form" does not really exist. It is all "virtual reality" taking place in the mind out pictured as real. For a moment, you couldn't alter the word "form" or type on the page. Your main document became inoperable because I again suspended your function in time and space. You wanted proof and this is it. You did disappear.

You are not form. Your "existence" does not depend on the five senses of the perceptive ego mind. Yes, they are necessary for you to carry on in this illusory world, but I can take you outside of all illusion. On the beach, you were bonded as One with Me so there is nothing to recollect because there was nothing to record or project. *HS, You are making this clear to me now. I have No sense of missing anything, no sense of loss about disappearing from a body or the universe. Death cannot be frightening and there is no point in even having someone describe a "Near Death Experience." I hand it all to You and leave You in charge.* I am in charge of the End of Time. It cannot be described, and is not related to the experience of what is called "death" which is just another manifestation of dreaming or dream states commonly believed to lead to Heaven or another lifetime. I am teaching you something else and it is related to Truth: have no need to explore the Wholeness of God Is. You are God and so your "experience" of your Self will *Be* God; not awareness or consciousness. Leave it at that. We are coming to the end, and you are getting accustomed to slipping out of what you once believed was reality. You are accepting your nothingness.

HS, this wipes out all attachment to form having any meaning. There is nothing of this ego life/mind that has value. It's all an illusion. You had to come this far to accept what I'm telling you. It shows you how much of the ego thought system you have deleted. You also know that ego defenses would not allow but very, very few to consider what is written here. The end of dreaming—the Awakening—is the "loss" of the world of form. It is about merging with Me. Mt has associated that with the bliss of a unity experience, but to be in Unity is not to be in form or in self-awareness. A good description would be the frames of time deleted from the filmstrip of your imagined life. You are not an individual, and are not separate from the Whole—God; Love. Smile at the Perfection of My showing you "whatever you need" to know that My Will prevails.

113

Un-Couching Fear

See innocence, and you will accept your own.

November 19, 2020

From Jo: *Years ago, I pretty much talked my husband Gary into buying a big purple couch for the living room. Although I loved the color, it turned out the couch wasn't all that comfortable. It was rarely used except by our cat, Rajah, who—as a youngster—decided to pee on it. Recently, I told Gary that we've had the purple couch "long enough" and I wanted to lighten up the space. The day before the couch was to be picked up and donated, I thought to give it a quick vacuum. As I took off the heavy cushions, I noticed some white residue where I must have missed cleaning, and wondered if the stain would prevent the guys from accepting it. I then recalled the last time Rajah had peed on it . . . a friend was staying in our guest room and Rajah had tried to hide under the bed. She screamed at him to get out, which scared him, and he frantically ran downstairs. A few minutes later I discovered he had peed on the couch, which he hadn't done for a long, long time. He was freaked out for most of her five week visit and I blamed her greatly for overreacting and traumatizing the cat. I am reluctant to invite her over again, and also because of the COVID-19. I asked the HS for help.*

Your reluctance about that same friend coming "in the door" is all about you—your projection that you should not enter the House of the Lord because you are a contaminant—guilty and deserving punishment. Forgive both of you. See her innocence, her unreality as a body and you will accept your own. Allow her to join you in the mind as equal, not a victim, although it has appeared that way with her many life challenges. Yes, she has been given many reasons to call on Me.

Yesterday I spoke with Margie, telling her about the hidden couch stain and how I could not bear the thought of "God's attack." Margie then shared a story of her cat Briley who belonged to her niece, but after seeing how the kitten had been neglected, Margie adopted Briley. Weeks after the adoption, Briley was looking out the window and saw the niece coming to the door for a visit. He totally freaked out. No wonder we think we can never go Home again. I could see, feel, and accept the depth of my own fear of being separate from God.

Today, when I finished cleaning the couch, I thought how guilt is discovered when our "cushions" are removed. When the guys came to pick it up, they said it would sell quickly because, "It's a good one!" They saw nothing wrong. I had to smile, knowing Nothing has ever happened to change that. Yes. All Is forgiven and released. For this I am forever grateful.

114

Vision of Death

The Light sees the Light.

December 23, 2020

Holy Spirit, help me today. I didn't sleep well until You wrapped me in peace and woke me at 6:45 am. I went to the rocks and dared to have a wish that maybe I could see the mating of the crabs. I brought along a Message from You to read and it happened to be about my death. After sitting for quite a long time, a large crab with beautiful red claws appeared, maybe three-and-a-half yards in front of me. We stared at each other . . . she with her bright black raised eyes. Very slowly she wended her way up and down the rocks getting closer and closer to me. When she came and sat on the tall rock a little over an arm's length in front of me, we stared at each other again. Amazing that she was not fearful.

After a while the crab slipped down between some rocks out of view and You told me to wait. I felt the stiffness of sitting so long so I stretched flat out across the rock in front of me and peered below me onto the sand, surprised to see that another crab was now on top of her. The white chamber under her body was open and receiving his insertion. They were in mating position about six feet away from me for about ten minutes. When I looked carefully, I could see her eyes had dropped down in her head and were no longer black, but transparent. She looked dazed, perhaps in sexual ecstasy, and did not move. Then her red claws met in prayer up in front of her face. The other crab had moved off her back and was foaming at its mouth. It then moved to the side but "my" crab didn't move. I guessed she had died, so I walked over and touched her legs. She was dead. This was a stunning symbol. HS, what is Your meaning?

You have been given another vision of your "death." It took place without pain or struggle in the position of union. When your time comes, it will be as easy as that. And yes, the crab came to you to die. That is what touches you. She let you see the intimacy of her death. She died in the sunlight. A large white cumulous cloud in the shape of a dove floated over you both, reminding you of the Baptism of Jesus, symbolized in the Bible by a white dove. *HS, she was a beautiful, determined crab as she made her way to me.* And this is how you have lived your life directed by Me. She was the perfect symbol of all the messages I have been giving you. Accept them. Know that you have died before you die in form. She made her way Home to Me, to you, because we are One. The Light sees the Light. Accept that now.

HS, why did my printer just stop printing and then the screen of my computer go black? I thought it died too. It seemed to be another mirror of death and I was quite concerned that I could not get it remedied because my tech friend is under quarantine. I wanted to reinforce the message with the crab. Death is death. It appears that the light is gone from the "screen" of what you call your projected life in a dream, like the vacant eyes of the crab, but in reality, the Joining in My Peaceful embrace has taken place. Celebrate the wondrous signs of this day. *Why did the crab die?* It was My Perfect timing for a Plan that makes no sense to the world. Rejoice that you were present to its death. You waited for it to dissolve into My Arms, and that was a blessing. We are Unified as One.

115

A Place of Transparency

See the impermanence; the transient nature of this world.

December 25, 2020

HS, I was just sitting on the rocks in sight of the dead crab from two days ago. The sun was up and it shined on a filament of spider extension between two rocks. I came to tears with the realization that my life on earth hangs by a thread. Yes, your web, your life/story, is undone, dismantled, and over, like the crumbled remains of the crab. You see that Everything is ephemeral . . . vanishing, disintegrating. You see the impermanence; the transient nature of this world. The shadows of tourists walking on the path pass in front of you reminding you of Plato's cave, but you see My Light in the rising sun. The time is near to join with Me. *HS, make this clear and deep for my grasping.* I will.

(Later) *Holy Spirit, I just went back to the rocks for sunset to see the dead crab. Pieces of it were scattered around but I found the eyes—clear globes for the setting sun to peer through. It again brought me to tears. We communed through those eyes once sparkling black. Why was I to find them?* It is how you find Me. You delete all the sights and sounds of ego perception and come to Me as a transparent vessel. This you have done, although you cannot claim or fathom it. The crab's eyes are your eyes given to Me, so through My Vision you can see clearly without obstruction. Those vacant, lifeless eyes are all that is left of mt. *Tears. There is nowhere to go and nothing to do now. I have handed over my shell to You. I have experienced my nothingness, knowing You are still there.* The eyes of earth are absent;

that you know. You have had to release all attachment to the body and ego self to come to this place of transparency. You wondered why today felt so "purposeless" believing it was because you had not been meeting with people, or feeling Christmas as a special day. But I had you where I wanted you. Nothing was wrong. The experience with the crab symbolized handing over your sight to Me, dying before you die, so I can live the Invisible Essence behind the mt character. This is My Christmas Gift to you. Cherish it.

116

Reorientation

Drop the idea that sights and sounds are outside of you.

December 27, 2020

From Jo: *After a night of dizziness, with images going "up" rather than sideways and around, like the usual vertigo experience, I woke up with a bit less of it, but still with some discombobulation. And no energy. Feeling very slowed down. Ok. That's the prescription for now. I was glad to remember that if I can taste and smell, I probably don't have COVID-19. The HS concurred. I asked Him to help me cope with feeling "off" and sat with Him quite a while in conversation. At the same time, the neighbor was pounding on the kids' treehouse and I was a bit distracted, wanting to have it quiet, but then recalled that the HS is everything. I realize that when I want to "get away" I am forgetting that He goes with me, unless I think I'm on I'm own. I then asked to be aware of "taking Him along" everywhere, and that's when the thought "nothing can Ever be separate" really solidified. When I am consciously aware that He is All of it, including me, I cannot be separate. So, HS, why the dizziness, today?*

I am in charge of your body, so have no fear. The reorientation of your mind also affects your brain and your physical stability. The world's dizziness is not catchy. Allow My Work and remind yourself that you are not a body but a free spirit. This is our goal. Allow Me to live you completely. You must stay in constant communication/connection with Me. I am everywhere and everything but you would still make things separate and then allow them to bother you. I am your neighbor's hammer. I am your off-kilter. Never separate Me from anything you see or hear.

I am your death and I am your life, breath, clothing, cat, family. All of it. See no differences in any form.

Symbols are My bag of tricks. My instruction. Dizziness seems like a power that overcomes Reason/Me until you accept that it *is* Me. Drop the world, drop the idea that sights and sounds are outside of you. When they are felt as real, you revert to being alone in a vulnerable body. Don't separate "Me" from "you." Stay joined, stay in trust, because we go Together; every step as One. Remember that I'm not only with you when you sit quietly; it's just easier to remember Me when you do. Continue to disregard any separate thoughts or actions. They cannot be real. Where you go, I go too. Keep that flame lit.

117

Only By Asking

Ask and I will give you each piece of information you need to further your awakening.

December 31, 2020

HS, I do believe I have come far, but mt did react when Jo told Meera that she shouldn't ask for specific things from You. What do You say? The relationship you each have with Me is the way into the depth of our union. You may bring everything to Me—all desires and dreams and anything that causes you upset or pain, such as body "alerts." Have no concern about the world or the outcome of any event. We forge ahead as planned and will come to a sweet conclusion. It is all in Divine Order. *Now the tears are flowing. I feel so loved and reassured and didn't even know I needed reassurance. Take me in Your Arms and lead me forward on the wings of Love. I surrender to Your Will.* Always call on Me for My Presence, Clarity, Peace, and Help.

(Later) *Jo said her ego was upset with me for disagreeing about not asking You for specifics.* The upset is really about her ego's belief that her "power" was stolen by your challenge. It is very threatened that you receive the messages so easily from Me. Not only do you have to be able to speak with Me and ask Me about everything, that's all you want in this life. I dictate to you when you accept My Voice as your own. I placed you here to do just that. This is an important lesson for many to hear . . . you all can access Me every moment to ask about any little or big thing and I will give you each piece of information you need in the exact timing to further your awakening.

From Jo: *Holy Spirit, not only did my ego react to mt who said I was "wrong" about not asking You for specifics, it still gets upset when she keeps saying . . . "Have you asked the Holy Spirit yet?" I know she is just trying to help and is not attacking me, but it feels like she doesn't think I know I need to ask, and doesn't trust me to do so. I ask You all the time for Your help, but I don't necessarily write it down or type it, although it's then harder to share Your answers. That's obviously a defense of mine. I know we can ask You anything about the dream for our learning and clarity, but not to ask for it to be changed or fixed, because that would mean we think it's real.* The reason Margie keeps after you is to remind you of the better way, which you do still need repeated. Remember, your ego wants people to bug you so it can get mad. The reason you get so upset is that you are coming from your wrong mind, which cannot tolerate Me. The remedy is to Put Me in Charge *before* impulsively responding. Establish Me in your right mind first and you'll just smile at what the ego would say. This way your mind is open and willing to hear her suggestions to Ask, without reacting.

Holy Spirit, I'm still listening to the ego rant, and am not ready to laugh yet, because of course, I can find truth in her words. I still want to be right and do it my way, even though I do know I must ask You about everything. Our Conversations are my daily Bread, helping me uncover all the places I resist the truth. And I know when I'm stuck, but when Margie insists that I ask You about my dreams, I must somehow think she has the "authority" to do so. I guess I believe it's "her way." I admit I resist asking You about most of my night dreams since I think I get a "good enough" idea about their meaning on my own, and am not always compelled. I forget that You can use everything to wake us up, and I do know I am sabotaging myself when I don't keep asking You for more clarity. Oh shit, what if I don't really want to wake up?!? I say that I am "perfectly satisfied" to hear You when I do, but that could mean I don't want to go further. Do I believe that You won't answer me clearly because, once again, that's "Margie's" way of interacting with You, but not mine? Then I still must not completely trust You. If I don't hear Your reply as quickly as I would like it "proves" that I am right about not deserving Your answers or Your help. Yikes! The ego is now claiming I am not worthy of You or Your Love. I know it's having a heyday with this. I Love talking with You, and I still have a lot of work to do.

Mt has been more disciplined to ask, ask, ask Me about the minutia, which are all symbols of awakening when interpreted with Me. Your only responsibility is to Me—your True Self. Be vigilant to what you are asked to do here in the world and check everything out with Me before you say yes. Old ways of being must go. Take some time off and be with this question, "What is your fear of asking Me about anything?" *Thank You, HS.*

From *ACIM*: *Yet only by asking will you learn that nothing of God demands anything of you. God gives; He does not take. When you refuse to ask, it is because you believe that asking is taking rather than sharing (T-11.VIII.5).*

118

Dig Deep

The belief in the separation from God is the source of all PTSD.

January 4, 2021

You are still wondering about the "message" of the PBS Masterpiece movie *Elizabeth is Missing,* which you watched last night. The main character, Maude, an eighty-year-old woman with Alzheimer's, was convinced that her elderly friend and neighbor, Elizabeth, had disappeared, but no one believed her. In Maude's deluded mind, her friend's strange vanishing was associated with the disappearance of Maude's own sister decades earlier, resulting in Maude's post-traumatic stress. It had been long repressed, but was now triggered. In the final scene, Maude's insistence that Elizabeth's garden be searched in the place where Maude had recently found her sister's mirror, led to the discovery of the sister's skull, buried deeply in the earth. Elizabeth, who had been in the hospital, was completely unaware of the role she had played.

The movie reflects the "deep digging" that Jo has been doing for the past few days to discover the source of her reluctance to ask Me about everything. When she finally spoke to you about her release of fear, you felt a beautiful sense of your own completion. The prodigal son had returned, and you had the tiniest taste of why I long for the return of all the many selves as the "Completion of God." Jo remained in touch with Me throughout as a "curious witness" of her ego thought system. She was totally willing to do the digging that would result in the uncovering of her repression of the original separation, asking Me to release it. The belief in the separation from God is the source of all PTSD, and the dissociation which follows is the "essence" of one's illusory life on earth. Nothing in the dream is accidental so there is really nothing to question about all the placements within it. Soon it will vanish just like the flame of a match when you blow it out.

Yesterday morning, you observed an oddly shaped pile of dried brown leaves beside the trash canister next to the elevator. You had seen it before, but this time you decided to pick it up. It surprised you to find the skull and full skeleton of a bird, which had been totally unrecognizable. It reminded you of the discovery of the skull in the PBS movie. Yes, it was stunning, but you totally accept this as the way the dream works.

Nothing is coincidental. Everything is presented in a "logical" unfolding for you to know that I am orchestrating every breath. You had to have this pairing, holding death in your hands, just like holding the eyes of the dead crab after witnessing its death. You are no different from Maude. Mt may appear "daffy" in the dream, but "you" are showing the world that deep down you know the truth, and it does set you free; the whole world with it. Stay with the power of this message. *HS, a tiny sparrow just flew into my living room through a small opening in the screen. What do You say?* You see the resurrection of the image of death. You now recall that after the movie you looked at your painting, *Beyond Form*—the skull of death with the dove of the Holy Spirit at the forehead to see that truth has come. You are saved and with you the world is brought to Light. You, Jo, and Meera are One Light and what one discovers you all embrace equally. Further.

119

Capitol Breach

I must be the only Interpreter of everything you see.

January 6, 2021

You just heard that the United States Capitol building has been stormed by protestors declaring the presidential election was stolen and demanding a recount of the votes. I told you that the political situation would get "worse before it gets better." The country is watching an idol being overturned; symbolic of the toppling of the ego thought system, which would rule the world. The "greatest, most powerful country in the world" must see the deception that clouds the mind, and former President Trump is a supreme example. I have humanity's attention now to see the need for resolution rather than a continued standoff between political parties. The world/the mind needs to be turned around; the battle must be seen and the choice for Me must be made. I AM the only Solution. Hear and know that I am behind the happenings of a world that make No sense, non-sense, to bring an awakening for those with ears to hear and eyes to see the Truth. You have no concern or fear because you trust that it is all in My Hands, serving My Plan for a "Grand Awakening," which will overturn all the idols in the made-up world. My Love and Constancy reign.

Yes, this is a Day of Gifts . . . the Epiphany, the gifts of the Magi, the gift of another stimulus for man to Wake Up. Love and Unity overcome falsehood. It is either chaos or clarity, darkness or light, and I must be the only Interpreter of everything you see. *HS, Zoe called as I was typing. She was sobbing at the evil portrayed in the destruction of the Capitol, saying "a barrier has been broken." I told her what You told me about the world needing a turnaround. She has the depth to see the darkest of the dark and also Your Light.* Zoe is My emissary and will speak to those she teaches from the understanding I have given you today.

From Meera: *Holy Spirit, please speak to me of the insurgence at the nation's capital. Was this event incited by Trump's continual lying about the election being a fraud?* Millions of people believe his lies and were duped, never conceiving of the extent of deception, although some have sensed that something is not right. As you watched the news, you sat without judgment, seeing all but uncontrollable rage being displayed. While talking with Margie you flashed back forty years ago to an experience of feeling something quite similar. At the time, you were studying bodywork and exercise. The owner of the school promised things you knew would never happen. As you sat listening to her speak, you found yourself enraged, and would "strangle" the lying woman if you didn't leave the room. You bolted for the door and shook with all but uncontrollable anger. *I felt like there was a volcano inside of me rumbling and about to erupt.* Yes, it was terrifying to think you had the thought, if not the capability, to murder someone. Today, while you watched the mob break windows and climb inside the Capitol building, you reconnected with the memory of what you experienced long ago and could understood the motivation of today's throng.

HS, "conspiracy theory" just popped into my head. We each have our own conspiracy theory against ourselves. The attack on the US Capitol is no different than our daily attacks on each other. At the original separation, you all were duped, lied to, and the trauma of believing the ego's lies resulted in imagining you would never be welcomed back into the Kingdom—ripped away from God, Truth, and Love. Your post-traumatic stress has held you captive in the mind long enough. Now is the time for you to look at all forms of deceit and forgive yourself and the brother for what never happened. Trump supporters are far from understanding that being lied to triggers separating from God. It is time to question the idols and find the better way. I am using these unsettling times to reorient people to a new direction, away from guilt, fear, and hatred, and towards love, joy, and peace. Stay with Me.

120

Depth of Denial

The world must be shown the extent of the ego's destructiveness.

January 7, 2021

Sit with Me now. You have seen how the ego rules, always looking for conflict, for someone to blame or attack. You are very familiar with the drama that ensues from all the world's stories. People are addicted to the projection screen they made, often symbolized by the Internet and media venues. Now we are turning that off. The ego hates stillness because in stillness it is absent. You think of Trump always needing to be at the center of the storm, like promoting the siege of the Capitol. He is desperately trying to overcome every obstacle to maintain the role of supreme power in the world. He had it and lost it and therefore his ego is screaming for attention; gathering forces to fight his battle to be on top. You see this perfectly out pictured on the world stage and are grateful to see it as a mirror of your own ego. Trump's election in 2016 made it clear that he stands for the ego thought system and is therefore fulfilling his role by showing the world the extent of his destructive will. There is no mistaking how the ego would take over man's consciousness to have its own ends met; to have life. God then becomes a distant thought in a mind consumed with drama and the ego's promise of a glorious future. Humanity must have the clearest out pictures of the ego's rule before an awakening can happen.

HS, I am getting the magnitude and intricacy of Your Plan and how our books are being used as instruments. This brings me to tears.

My eyes are opening . . . I made the dream, I see my ego out pictured in this world, in Trump, and I also know the solution—You, my Self, the Christ—the same for all who stormed the Capitol. You are The Capitol. The One and Only. No other exists. The pictures are now filling the mind screens of the world's population as they filled my mind this morning. This example is the clearest ever. I am almost giddy with Your clarity today. We See with Your Vision the truth of what is happening—bringing light to a world submersed in a black nightmare. I stand above the battleground with You and watch it all unfold, impersonally as a witness to report at Your request.

121

No Heaven on Earth

Only the mind given fully to Me will wake up.

January 10, 2021

HS, You had informed me that I would not be watching "60 Minutes" tonight even though I was looking forward to it. I couldn't understand why until I saw April walking toward me on the beach and knew I wouldn't make it home in time for the program. She said she is still standing up for Trump and that the Great Awakening is coming. I kept repeating to her that there is only one way to Awaken—through direct access to Your Voice. On some level I think she gets it. You were being Spoken and you were clear. It will sink in. You stood your ground; My Ground. April had to deny the Christ supremacy in herself to choose the ego's path—an out picture of all lifetimes rolled into one. Your Light is almost blinding because it is OWG/Me. You must be blocked out for her to survive as an ego character. Trump gives permission for the ego to rebel, to falsify the clear "election" for Truth, Unity, and Peace. In time, April will look at her own ego's power represented by Trump. Your work is to just show up and remind all beings of the Christ Light in them. Her eyes will be opened in My time.

HS, I can hardly identify with the vessel mt and must look at her as just a symbol for the Light. Is it true that fear of being "blinded" keeps many away from me? Yes. *I get that. The Light either opens or closes a door to their Inner Light.* This is the script that April has chosen for this life and you, as My symbol, cannot really be rejected. But April is afraid of acknowledging the truth that her idol is false, so she has to shut out My Light. It has nothing to do with mt. I have left a door open where April can see the truth/Me in the Light you shed. She does hear your guidance, although she lives in the lie of the "reality" of the ego's deceptions. I am still with her and that is what is confusing for her, but she has not asked Me directly about Trump and his role in the world. Yes, I am available in the mind of every dreamer.

I want you to know that April is destined and determined to awaken from the dream of her attachment to the dichotomy, because to take "either side" is to remain embattled, which will keep her forever in hell. Hell is clearly depicted in the world with the division now made so clear with the chaos. The "Great Awakening"—the remaking of the world—is greatly misconstrued. It is not "waiting on the other side" and will not change the entire world for the better. There is no world. True Awakening is where each soul sees its Self as the owner and carrier of the Light. There will be no heaven on earth. Mt/April are nothing but projections of the separation with different belief systems. She will awaken, but first she must see that the world won't change. Only the mind given to Me will wake up. Keep removing the barriers to Truth. All denial must be released to awaken fully.

122

Primal Scream

The intensity of our union always invokes fear in your ego; fear of Love.

January 12, 2021

HS, I feel like I let out a "primal scream" in my dream last night when I saw three hazy pencil sketches of what I believed was the face of the devil on a distant wall. (At some level it seemed to be April's face.) Then, right above me, a man came out on the balcony. Somehow, he also represented those hazy images, but I had no other clue about him because he was just a dark figure. When I saw him on the balcony, I fell to the floor and let out a blood curdling scream, which felt like a "literal" experience. In this lifetime, I have dealt with that kind of response in which a patient reenacts a particularly disturbing past experience and expresses repressed anger or frustration through spontaneous screams, hysteria, or violence.

It *was* a primal scream and you heard yourself make it in the dream. It was unassociated with emotion but was the most powerful scream you could imagine. I wanted you to scream in the face of the devil. You met your own devil . . . the ego thought system "face to face" and responded to the terror of that with a scream. It was beyond what you would call fear because you did not feel it in your body. It was also beyond the body because it was primal, before birth, and came from the depths of your being. It was the recognition of the choice for separation, but without having any data for what an "ego" was or where it would lead you. Now you see the devil, ego, for what it is—Nothing—just an image on a wall or a dark figure on a balcony. In your night dream, those images were enough to return you to the memory of leaving Home, which you now can release at a new level. Of course the ego does not want you to see the significance of this experience, but that is why it is essential that you bring it to Me now.

(Later) *HS, I'm so annoyed by the loud and noisy backup alerts from the trucks, and also the blowers and lawn mowers and all the beach goers.* You are still reacting to what almost shook you awake last night—a scream of bloody rage at yourself for leaving the Kingdom, for which you would attempt to destroy yourself and the universe. This time, you faced it and let it all out; a powerful expression that needed to happen. You will see why. *Did my scream also relate to what is happening in the world right now?* Yes, your ego is screaming at your recognition of what you "created," which therefore marks its death. It has been confronted and is murderously furious.

But HS, I don't feel anything now. That is because you rest in My Peace above the battleground. Remain untouched by the trauma and chaos of the world. This was just the day for the scream to take place. *Why am I so tired tonight?* You have placed yourself in full rejection of the ego, which takes an emotional toll. This is its reaction. *HS, have I finished what I needed to learn vis-à-vis the primal scream?* You approached the depth, and there is more to come. Have no concern. *Why did I think of April as the devil?* You clearly see how her ego operates as it undoes her communion with Me. You do not judge her, but will nudge and guide her. She will wake up. It's in her DNA. As you see, this work with her has taken you to an unknown place in your mind. It will have an effect, which you have no capacity to imagine.

From Meera: *HS, what do You say about my reaction when Margie shared her "primal scream" dream and message?* The moment of separation holds a most egregious experience. The mind cannot conceive of separating from love; potentially never to reunite with it ever again. Removing dense layers of belief to approach this is not for the meek. You three have dedicated your lives to unlocking this treasure chest and are not quite finished. Stay as close to Me as possible. *HS, now I am tearing up.* You know Me. You trust I never leave you. We are One. The intensity of our union always evokes fear in your ego; fear of Love. The more the character fades away, the more merged you are with Me. The less fear and hate, the more the love. *HS, I give You my resistance to love. Please help me navigate the way back to You.* The gap is closing.

123

Affirming the Truth

You must hold fast to "purifying" your beliefs.

January 13, 2021

Holy Spirit, I just read an email from April stating that "my" HS is the wrong HS, i.e., some form of ego projection. Even my writing is shaky now as are my whole insides. What do You say? The primal scream has taken place and now the upset has followed. Feel the fear and move on fearlessly with Me. *But April is indicating You are lying to me. I now have tears recalling the betrayal of other friends, and also the betrayal of Jesus by Judas and Peter.* Yes, you know the story well; all reminders of the betrayal of God that you have forgiven, along with your Self. This is the freedom you now experience. You see April's betrayal of Me—you—and forgive her, knowing that I have a greater Plan beyond the fighting between ego factions and personalities.

I am operating in the mind at a far greater level than you could possibly imagine, but you can call what is "happening" an "Armageddon" and the interception of the ego's battle for supremacy. You and April are central in exposing that battle, just in different ways. Let it ride for now until I tell you to take action. I am all that matters. *What about Meera and Jo?* They are your/My supporters, and verifier of My Messages. Our books affirm My Truth, which is supported by the endorsers. *How do I answer April?* You can mention Chapter 17 in the *Course* about the Holy Relationship and leave it at that. I will be there and will make the path clear. Stand back now and give Me Full Reign. *Will do, HS. Thank You for this stunning gift to bring light to a divided world.*

From Meera: *I asked the HS about April and this was given . . .* April has been duped. Releasing the ego/devil to embrace the light will be a harrowing feat; a traumatic experience for her. Trust that you all will come out the other side stronger, grokking this journey at a new depth. Margie is feeling closer to reversing the original separation than ever before, and you and Jo are close behind. You must hold fast to "purifying" your beliefs. I have loved and nurtured you three through forever. Your discipline of Asking has increased in strength over time, especially recently. Margie breathes My Breath; separated only by a thread. Neutralizing your thinking so you can embrace all that I present to you takes energy and concentration. This is about coming to nothingness, disappearing, reuniting into the One. *HS, I feel a bit numb.* The magnitude of this cannot be understood from the dream state. Stay alert. There is nothing to fear. The Beloved is very near.

124

Teamwork

Ask Me for the meaning of absolutely everything that gives a moment's pause.

January 19, 2021

You have watched on television the preparations for Joe Biden's Inauguration tomorrow and also heard that the Capitol building is hunkered down in preparation for another possible attack. The president-elect appears calm and reasonable. He will welcome the country into a covenant of love, which reflects his relationship with Me. Be assured that I will be guiding him in his leadership of the country. A healing in the one mind will take place under My Auspices. Biden's light is strong, as is the vice president's, and this "scenario" has to be played out at this time in the universe. We are One Mind/One Sonship, but duality in the split mind has to be brought to the surface so it can be healed. Let it unfold as I Will, and watch it all through My Vision above the battleground. You are My witness.

Now you recall your night dream where you were walking midday in a rocky desert with no supplies, no food, or water. Your shoulders were getting burned from the sun and someone appeared with sunscreen. I will manifest what you need for the asking as the end nears. Have no concern as none of it is real. In another dream, you were taking wedding photos of Zoe, but when you woke up, you realized you had no camera in that dream and that she was only an image in front of you; just a projection of yourself as a dream character. This reflects the disorientation you now feel in your daily life, that you aren't really "here" in this nation dislodged from knowing what is true and what is a lie. The PBS news hour discussed the same thing; what Trump's "legacy" will be after leaving office.

We are at the End of time, the End of dreaming, and yes, you are still aware of your human condition. But now you know it is not real. You know you are being lived by Me because you have given your whole life to Me. There is nothing else to know or do except to show up where I place you and teach this: to "Ask Me for the meaning of absolutely everything that gives a moment's pause." That is how the three of you have reached this point of understanding. You gave your imagined lives to Me, and I direct each thought and action—day and night. This is how our books will have a role in the healing of the nation/nations. Have confidence that "our team" will make a difference.

125

Power of One

Embrace the Sonship with Love and take it in.

January 20, 2021

HS, I am relieved that the Presidential Inauguration happened so beautifully and peacefully, but my real joy was writing with You after having a dream of being married to Biden. We were walking side by side down the enclosed wooden staircase in my home where he was staying. I knew we were married and felt a peaceful equality; a very strong sense that we'd get to know each other over time. I was happy and accepting. You awakened me at 5 am so we could write for forty-five minutes before the Inauguration started at 6 am, Hawaii time. What do You say?

We are joined in Holy Matrimony. You see your marriage to all the Sonship, all your selves, in this dream image. Biden has "married" the whole country and would unite, with Me, all the selves on the battlefield—the ego mind/dream of separation. In your night dream, you are paired with him as you walk down the stairs "from the podium." You know each other as the Christ, joined for all time, and at the time of Jesus. Your mission is equal, and you feel it deeply as you accept him as your "husband" in a gentle union. He also represents Me in My acceptance and constancy. You, the Self, represent Oneness with God—the extension from a mind unified in Me. I encompass the whole world in My Love. This is the bottom line.

(Later) *HS, I feel the peace of joining with Biden in the mind, like with You, and that it will develop and grow in time. I honor him as president and as my equal along with others. Our joined heart is compassionate. I feel warmly to my "new husband," accepting what is.*

I have no ego need or agenda. There is no world because Your Presence is everywhere. Does this dream join OWG with the new president? Yes, it is a strengthening of My Presence for the Whole mind because you are both joined in the same purpose: to awaken the world to the Light. Today you saw Love manifested and extended to the world in the Inauguration Ceremony. You were seeing My Face of Love in a time of overcoming the darkness. Embrace the Sonship with love and take it in. I have opened the heart/mind of the country to receive this.

HS, at the end of the Ceremony, I noticed the image of the rotunda on the dome of the Capitol over a background of blue sky and "saw" the cover of the OWG book given to me in the dream I had requested from You on 8/8/2012. I knew then that the rotunda symbolized the Unity of humanity. This was mirrored and demonstrated today. You witnessed the Power of OWG as originally intended—to see the integration within your Self of Love and Unity in My Presence. We are all One with God. *HS, this message seems to me like the most meaningful experience of the whole day!*

126

Right Side Up

I am your Only Reality in this "godforsaken" world.

January 31, 2021

Holy Spirit, thank You for this beautiful morning on the rocks . . . seeing the maroon anemone with coral tentacles and the crab that touched my hand then sat just five inches from my nose. I'm now recalling my night dream where an enormous sea turtle had turned upside down, right over a trickling creek that was less than one foot wide. I implored others to turn it back over but no one would, leaving my "mission" incomplete. What do You say? We are looking at mt from above the battleground and her confusion about the upside-down world she made. Stand back and smile.

What about the huge turtle I wanted to turn right side up? That was your projected image of a powerful being out of its Home element—you!—too big for a little creek and outside the Ocean of Being. You are not a body and that is the discomfort of "living" in a world of death. Even though you are driven to "right" the turtle, you will never fit into this world. You are waking up to see this cannot be your true Home. Your body does not belong to this world. In the beginning, you renounced your True Nature, which is God and Light, then found yourself in darkness and pain. Mt will never navigate this world with ease. Nothing here can reverse the story of suffering. The discomforts of the body are a projection of being out of your element—Divine Love. Only Waking Up will turn you Right Side Up to Me. I am your Only Reality in this "godforsaken" world. Forgive mt for her dream, her mistaken beliefs, and return to Me. I will always right you.

127

Birthing the World

Pain comes from attachment.

February 4, 2021

From Jo: *Right before I woke up this morning, I had a dream of standing in a large room like an empty cafeteria with a tile floor and some trash cans. Only a few people were visible, standing very far away, and perhaps it was my husband Gary who was near me. All of a sudden, I looked down at the floor and realized that some watery blood, just a little, had apparently come out of my body, letting me know I would be giving birth in just a few seconds. I wasn't expecting that but I crouched down, figuring I would just squat like many women do around the world. Right then I felt something coming out of my birth canal and saw the head of a small baby. I reached down to gently pull his shoulders through as he easily slipped into my hands without a sound; also, with no pain or discomfort on my part. As I held him up, I saw how long his legs were and thought he looked like those toy rubber chickens we used to see on TV. I looked into his face, not sure whether or not he was breathing (he seemed like a he), and a woman from across the room said to rub his back to get him to respond. He was very still with open eyes and a plain look. I had absolutely no reaction about having given birth. I hadn't known I was pregnant and only had a twinge of thinking that this event was a little odd. I don't recall seeing any umbilical cord, and I woke up without any emotion at all. What do You say, HS?*

The birth of the dream of separation—the world—was just as "unplanned" as the birth in your night dream. Both were an effortless extension of your own mind that took form. It "came from you" but now you are shown you have no attachment to it;

no interest in "another lifetime" or need to "mother" the earth anymore. When you woke up from the dream this morning, you experienced no sense of loss or any thought of what happened to the baby, so it disappeared. You felt impersonal, with no regret. Yes, the dream is over when you don't attach. Pain comes from attachment. Even your own back pain was gone this morning. The dream world and its characters are nothing you desire.

Now you think of your "actual" pregnancy in 1978, when you were excited to be pregnant after many months of trying. Soon after you gave birth to your son, you were "fulfilled" yet overwhelmed at the thought of this huge responsibility now placed upon your life. You believed you had both "gained and lost" at the very same time—you got what you had asked for, but lost the "you" that had been free. You unconsciously believed you could never be "you" again so you did whatever you could to regain some control. Your decisions were often selfish and your feelings numb. Now you fully realize that Nothing can ever satisfy in this dream world; it holds nothing you could want. Everything here is an illusion and the script is over. It always "works out" because it already has.

128

No Charge

I am the only Answer and the only Source of Clarity.

February 8, 2021

I have taken you beyond the world. This you realized after sitting on the rocks at 8:45 this morning and leaving at 10:20. It was the latest you have ever stayed and the sun was high in the sky. You watched the crabs sitting in their appointed places for about an hour, and then we left. I did "disappear you." It was the perfect timing for our jaunt outside this universe. Nothing happened of which you are aware and nothing was missed on earth. It was a replication of your night dream experience of being completely detached from the dream script you made. You realize there is nothing of this world that holds you. Last night you dreamed you were compelled to pay your taxes at a little shop where you begged the owner to accept them. Instead, a fairly large woman behind the counter handed you 1100 dollars as a refund, but you were not quite sure for what. Later, when you asked for My interpretation, I said you have been given compensation for something you are unaware of "purchasing"—your investment in a world that never materialized in reality. Now "we are even." Nothing ever happened, just like this morning, when you "lost" half an hour yet suffered no loss. You have never had to "pay" for the dream you made up, or pay with your life. There is no life to pay for. It is a story you agreed to host and now it is over.

(Later) Today on your rocks you experienced another "disappearance" and now you've just seen it mirrored in the movie *2001, A Space Odyssey*. You were surprised when the spaceship was lost and the computer commander Hal was "deleted" by the only one remaining in charge. You recall there were two periods of a black screen Intermission during the movie. Yes, the void was symbolized, along with the deletion of Hal's ego voice. I am the only Commander and I am reinforcing that now. You are willing to fall into the void that takes you out of this world. Your readiness comes from the deletion of your ego thought system, which always feeds you misinterpretations. I am the only Answer and the only Source of Clarity. Seek Me and no other. We go together beyond time and space.

129

One Powerful Self

I *Intend* My Light to shine on all the trials and tribulations of humanity.

February 12, 2021

Holy Spirit, I am embracing Your many gifts today, including the video of my turtle book "Finding 'Oli," *the Finnish Translation of OWG Book 1, and the Audible for Book 1, voiced by Marion Whatley; all happening in the last week. It is beyond my capacity to take it in with the level of gratitude it deserves. When I first met Marion, who came to Maui to attend a Gary Renard workshop, years ago, she told me even then that she is to be the voice for the audio version of our books. Today, on the phone, she said that at age six, at school, she "sang with the angels"— the most divine song she has ever heard. I guess I am finally grokking that I was to scribe the OWG books. I know that sounds foolish to say after six books are out with a seventh on the way. I do find it interesting that these gifts are appearing simultaneously with the Trump impeachment trial. I remember how You had me attend the Federal trial in Oahu in 2019, seating me right behind the defendant to spread Your Light. Tears. HS, I am honored to serve You in every way. I just heard . . .* "your light burns so brightly." *I guess that must be the case. I can't deny the intricacy of Your amazing Plan to bring me to Maui with all the players, and later today we have a Zoom meeting with the Avocado Group to review the new website they have developed for us.*

You have been given a multiple "impact" of events to clarify your role in this dream of "salvation." The timing of seeing My words go out in three different venues, from Maui to Finland and beyond, makes the point clear that My timing is not accidental.

Receiving the audio, the video, and even the new website today is a statement of completion. I am notifying the world stage and the one mind that I *Intend* My Light to shine on all trials and tribulations of humanity to one day make the final choice. Your contribution is monumental because it is the continuation of the principles of *ACIM*. I am telling you the truth and with the happenings of the day, it can't be denied. Your ego is essentially gone so you can accept this without rejection or resistance.

OK, HS, but I really don't feel any different. I am just here to follow through with Your Plan. Go with Me throughout the day and shine My Light. That is your only task in the dream and the purpose of the books going into the world. Leave it at that. You just had a flash of insight that we are "One Powerful Self" fulfilling a purpose beyond the limitations of the dream. You have no idea how I am using this to feed the world right now. The division must be healed and *OWG* is the glue in the mind that can do the healing. The three of you have come to hear My Voice and are willing to broadcast My Light. The resistance is gone because you know the importance of shining brightly right now as you let the remaining veils go. We are One.

Thank You, Holy Spirit, for this confirmation. It is the moment of 11:11 and we celebrate the dissemination of Your Word! This has been a big day and I am grateful. I rely on You. Tears. I feel You as my place of rest and comfort and trust. The world is gone but You are here with me now. You feel the depth of the offerings of Love coming through My words being placed in the mind and on the planet, which is in jeopardy of losing its Soul. Yes, I mean that.

130

Refreshed

Hold on to the knowing that we are a unit of Oneness and All That Is.

February 14, 2021

When I first arrived at the beach this morning, I sensed mt's nothingness, her flimsiness on the rocks. Then after what seemed like fifteen minutes, it felt as if a shift had happened . . . the children I had just seen on the beach were now in the water, and "I" was feeling whole, solid, and integrated like a monolith. It was as if I were renewed in what I would call "missed time." What do You say? Yes, indeed, I again took you from the world of form. This time you noticed the shift and could identify that it had taken place because it felt as if something "reorganized" like a computer refreshing. You can use the word "solidified," which does not refer to disappearing, but to your composition of Unity with Me. That is what is solid. We are One; stable in our Beingness. *Yes, HS, that makes sense. I am not questioning our unity as OWG. That is what You are showing me. We are One and the form disappears and does not matter. But we are beyond form. Thank You.*

Time is gone, meaningless . . . a day, or fifteen minutes, or lifetimes; all the same. Remember that we are deleting "future" lifetimes along with the past. In the moment of disappearance, it is all gone. There is only the Nothingness of the Now. All and Nothing. The Void. On the rocks, you left past and future and that is why you felt refreshed; stripped of all form, image, or thought. With Me, you have gone beyond form, time, and space so there can be no remembrance; no perception of missing out. Nothing is missed because the dream is nothing. I hold all of this in the Mind of God; beyond the mind of a self to understand. Let it all go and celebrate that we have joined in Union; One with God—that is My Valentine's gift to you this day. You now carry My Light forward through time, healing the misperceptions of form because you have lost all identification with the mt self. Your mind allows the Light of My Presence to hold the space of the dream and all the dreamers.

Today you surrendered to the disappearing and would not inhibit it. You are willing to "leave the world" whenever I call. This is a major step of letting go. You have given mt to Me and have no concern for that body/image on the rocks. You are beyond attachment and ego perception is deleted. I am in charge. Hold on to the knowing that we are a unit of Oneness and All That Is. Actually, you were being shown that you are returning to the beginning, before time. This morning, when I told you that mt is fading, it was the prelude to what took place on the rocks. You *did* disappear from the dream with no consequence to your body, and were sitting comfortably on your rock when you "came back." Do remember this: Images are *never* real. You can appear to be sitting on a rock, but you were never sitting on a rock because you were never really there as a true Christ Self.

These "experiences" are all about the manipulation of images, but they are nothing. Know that Life as Me is Beyond form. *HS, I love that I disappeared with You today and it affirms the unreality of this dream world.* Yes. You three all embrace that this world is collapsing and that you are insignificant as an ego player. You each accept the roles you've been given even if at times you have wanted to run away and end it all. It is not yet time to completely vanish from the dream, but each day you are getting closer. Your disappearances will happen again because it is a part of the preparation for the final dismissal of this dream nightmare. Persist with Me. It will all fall into place. You'll smile at the dream you made, then go out like a flash. Have patience. I hold your hand and take you through the last hoops.

From Jo: *There is something in your Margie-mind that so easily accepts this state of disappearance. Some kind of readiness, surrender, or just the great willingness to trust. Thank you for bringing more Light in!*

131

With the Whales

There is no kingdom, and you are the God that never left Itself.

February 21, 2021

Holy Spirit, thank You for this day. In the script, I am going on a whale watch with Zoe and am shaking with fear. I give it to You and ask for Your Peace throughout my being. You have it. Always. *What is this excursion really for?* You are going with Me in the mind to explore the unseen depths of your soul. You have been in the "belly of the whale" with Me as Jonah, as Lewis, and as Zoe. They represent your "Moby Dick"—the whale that must be slayed—the self of shame, regret, and hatred. You are but an image of a soul that believes it is lost in the sea of nothingness, separated from its eternal Home.

This is a symbolic day and it is necessary that you willingly take this journey with Me. Your anxiety and fears are meaningless. We are together and all else is a mirage. Remember that. "Whales and Zoes" are of the mind; images you created to scare you. So yes, we call in Ahab and Jonah this morning to represent the eternal suffering of man who believed he left and betrayed the Kingdom of God. But there is no kingdom, and you are the God that never left Itself. God could never split off any part of Itself. The Universe/Sonship is one undivided Whole. Again, you will spend time with Zoe who is angered that she can never really join with you and become united. Zoe is your out picture in the dream, and you long for union with her as she does with you. When you are brought together, it is to heal the separation in your mind and in the world. All your work here is about the Return to Union with Me, your Self. Rest in Me today knowing nothing can go wrong. Come what may, I am in charge, and I embrace you both as One Self, One with God.

(Later) *Holy Spirit, You gave us the perfect day . . . smooth ocean, clouds for shade then sun for warming, and whales all around . . . a mother, baby, and escort in the bluest water. I enjoyed seeing them and being close, but it does not move me as does seeing the sparkles topping the waves like stars—the pathway to heaven. I sobbed as I focused on You. I should be awed by whales but it was the momentary stars of light that touched my heart. Now I have the thought that I was just "pasted" onto that scene; a cutout like the faces on Zoom. I don't belong on this earth. It was passing me by on the boat. Zoe and the others were very kind and I felt totally comfortable and unselfconscious exposing my naked body after shaking from the cold of the water. You orchestrated it perfectly for me. Back home now I feel disoriented and displaced, similar to disappearing but more pronounced. I'm glad I went and do not need to go again.*

You are right where I want you—unattached to this world. There is nothing here that attracts you. The whale watching was no more than watching crabs on the rocks. *On the trip, I got to be with mt's body, its frailties, and forgive it. I also welcomed Zoe's lavish praise about how agile I am. She said what a great job I did snorkeling and I enjoyed her tenderness as she fed me and offered warm clothes. What about the thought of just being a "sticker" placed on the day?* That says it all. You were there and left. What matters is your Communion with Me before, during, and after. Embrace My Presence as "who" you are, and the rest is just a whale of a story.

132

Done with the Hunt

When you surrender, you have no idea what is taking place on a deeper level of the mind.

February 22, 2021

Holy Spirit, what was Your purpose for me going on the whale watch yesterday? The joining with Zoe was a completion of a sacred contract that was to happen now. You joined with her in love and gratefully allowed her kind ministrations. You are paired in the mind and you accept her fully as your Self. When you surrender and do what I ask, you have no idea what is taking place on a deeper level of the shared mind. Your initial fear was of being subsumed by Zoe, eaten by Moby Dick and Jonah's whale, but this time you were vulnerable in form and she could "tender" you. You entered her kingdom/whaledom willingly. Of course, this means you entered Me—your Whole Self with trust that I would tend to you and override your fears.

Much happened on your outing and there is no need to go whaling again. You welcomed each other into your hearts without rejection. She is the Self you had disowned and forsaken, but yesterday, you could be nothing but grateful for her support. In that moment, she became your Self/Me and we were One. *HS, I now feel a real closeness with Zoe and want to stay neutral and impersonal. We do love each other in the dream. Have I severed emotional ties with her as You willed?* Yes. You saw the day with her as symbolic and let her know of that importance. You even offered her My messages, an offer that is staying with her on the level of a holy relationship. That is where we were headed. Now keep it there. *HS, I have no desire to go whaling again. The "whale watch" represented the end of my search. You are found and Zoe is love.* You have found the whale and are done with the hunt. You have come Home to Peace, to Me, and never need to search again.

(Later) *Zoe came over to me on the beach tonight. I feel how we are in the same place—a blank slate to be open to however we are done. I told her about Joining with her as the Self, and completing my Mission. She got very teary and told me not to go/die before she does, and to give lots of warning, months before I depart. She said she can't imagine coming to the beach without me here. We hugged and affirmed our love for each other.* You have been Zoe's model and partner and she knows you are ultimately paired. She has reached the point of acceptance that I am her Life. This is the goal.

133

Pain of Sleep

Own your story and let it go.

April 3, 2021

We are One Self. That is All. That is the end of "it" . . . the end of the world. Last night you dreamed of experiencing a searing leg cramp that made you cry out, but when you woke up, you sensed the aftermath of the dream pain as only a very slight twinge. You then knew you had never really screamed or had any real pain. This is about the pain of sleep. It is *all* about sleep. The pain of the separation is out pictured in the dream both day and night. It's *all* dreaming. The pain and suffering of the Easter story is the heartache of the Sonship for the belief they left Heaven; the manifestation of guilt and the desire for atonement. As you have read in *ACIM,* "The Son of God was never crucified." There was never a "Jesus" and the whole world is a made-up story, now coming into the Light. In your night dream, you "felt the pain" but woke up to find it was really nothing. You own your story and you let it go.

Holy Spirit, why did I have the cramping dream? This was your "proof of dreaming" because that pain did not wake you up! No one came to your door hearing any yelling. It did not happen in "reality" but you still have a lingering "body memory" of it. *Why, HS?* You get it deeper yet that nothing here has ever happened. It is all a story. *Mt isn't real.* Night and day are the same—nothing. The crucifixion was just a dream, but became "real" in the shared mind of the Sonship that believed it was separate from God. So, there can be no guilt. The crucifixion did not "happen." Mt was never born and she'll never die. She is OWG in the Mind. Now. Our Communion tells the truth.

No one, as an ego character, wants to release their suffering because it is their "payment" for believing in the reality of the dream; for choosing the sleep of Satan, the serpent, and the idols, not unlike the golden calf that would lead them from their self-inflicted hell. In your night dream, you "felt" the searing pain and it stimulated an after-effect in your imaginary body. The dream must center on pain and conflict for it to "work" and it will not end until you see that neither day nor night dreaming is true. *HS, I feel the cramp resolving.* Yes, the pain of this life dissolves as you see it for what it is and offer it to Me.

134

Easter Story

The tomb was always empty.

April 4, 2021

You have had an "illuminated insight" that has taken you to a deeper level of knowing this world is a dream. Last night, I led you to watch a love story by Rabindranath Tagore. Although you couldn't keep up with the subtitles, you saw that it was about a man who loved two women, and those women became friends. The scenes you watched before going to bed centered on four days of love making after the first marriage. Early this morning you woke up to loud love making in the condo next door, which shook your shared wall and bed. You knew there was no coincidence in the pairing of these two experiences. Both were showing you the compelling power of the desire to replicate, to combine in sexual union. It is what keeps the dream going because the attraction, the chemistry between bodies and brains cannot be denied or even ignored. Attraction to the "other" is what creates the desire to return to dreaming, lifetime after lifetime. You observed it all without judgment, which was the whole purpose. I am pairing this experience with yesterday's message about the pain of a night dream being the same as the pain of the dream of day.

Everything is a Dream. You do get it. You are clear that Jesus is a dream character no different from mt, and that the Easter story is just that—a story. The stories of the world are all arranged to "lead you Home"—to wake up as One Self. But there is no Home, just as there is no World. There is No divine "welcoming center" in a dream of made-up selves. You are already Home,

OWG, as One Self in Communion with Me. We are not "off to heaven." The idea of another realm or special place must go. It is all story. This is the disappearance—rapidly moving beyond belief in the dream. *HS, this does not feel like a loss at all.* Yes, because you have stepped out of the world. I present the Truth. Jesus was never crucified because he was never real. He was a figure in a dream of redemption and release from the self-made hell of this illusory world; the savior, idol, rising up to "heaven." None of that is true. The tomb was always empty. You have only been living in a tomb of sleep, a hollow shell called a body. You accept this without resistance. *Yes, HS. This is my awakening and further release from the dream of separation. I let it all go because Only You are Real.*

135

The Burning

Let Me reinterpret every aspect of your imagined physical life.

April 29, 2021

You are All the Same Self and the body is not real. *HS, I know that is true, and yet I am still upset over the constant burning of my lips over the past several years. Is it the burning desire to speak of You and from You and to tell Your story?* Yes, you are speaking from Me and your lips are the gateway. Use every "annoyance" for gratitude that I speak from those sacred lips. The ego uses them to upset you, to make you believe you are a real body. I am the Only One that is Real, and I burn with Desire for our Reunion beyond form. Let the lips burn. They open the way to My Presence and appearance in the world; the gate to the Inner Sanctum of our Union. Accept that as the solution and look at the symbolic nature of everything.

The ego would defile the most sacred external manifestation of My Presence from which My words pour forth. Treasure your burning lips like the burning bush, and My command to Mohammad: "Recite." The lips express My Wonders. Do not judge or fear them. Praise My Lips. They are Mine and belong to Me. Treat them with Love. You are not diseased or malnourished. Accept what is. I am in charge. You see how the ego wants to attack by having you think you are damaged, inadequate, and in need of a doctor. I am the only Doctor. Turn to Me. *HS, I see how strongly my ego is wanting to make this body discomfort real. Release me from that ego desire.* You had to see this to now release it. Let Me reinterpret every aspect of your imagined physical life. The burning itself is imaginary, but is a sign of My Presence at the gate to full Health and Wholeness. Praise My Power and Love to speak through lips given to Me.

(Later) *Holy Spirit, I have been feeling peace and joy since this early morning's message.* You are tuned into Me because you gave your greatest upset to Me and fully received My Loving answer. Your burning lips have been a great concern, yet you didn't mention them to the dermatologist two days ago. I wanted you to come to Me for the solution; not new lip balms, or raw aloe vera juice. And I gave you from the Depths of My Heart an answer that has filled you with Joy. Now you wonder why you have resisted asking Me for years about your almost constant obsession with that problem. It was time, and yes, you do ask about everything, but not your mouth because it is "too close" to Me and is the threshold of your entrance to Heaven.

HS, yesterday I was making preparations for my future cremation. Did that set up my willingness to finally ask You about my burning lips? Yes, and last night your friend Marie told you of the piles of dead bodies from COVID-19 in India waiting for the pyre. That was also a sign. Now you are happy, ready, and willing to go all the way to the deletion of mt 's "life." You can already feel the joining that will happen at the canoe "ash ceremony" with all your friends; a celebration of uniting in spirit. The Mind rejoices with the Return of the Son. We are all One Self and this is how you know our Unity.

136

In the Oven

Look at everything as a message of Love from Me.

April 30, 2021

You have no agenda today other than *taiji* on the beach. Let the day flow minute by minute with Me. I know the way and you do not need a specific directive. In last night's dream you seemed to be floating in space until the interior of an old-fashioned gas oven, like your mother's, came into view. Your "head" was in the oven, and you were holding a lit match, but you were not a body. You were "inside the thought" of your own cremation. This need not be explained, just as your daily life does not need definition and you do not need a detailed message from Me every day.

But HS, I want to sit with You and focus on only You. We can focus on each other no matter where you appear to be. Think of Me while you are doing *taiji* . . . as you walk the beach . . . as you do your computer work. I will give you messages as necessary, but I do not want you to rely on receiving them daily. They are the frosting of life but not its sustenance. I sustain you with every image you see in this beautiful world. Look at everything as a message of Love from Me . . . the rainbow over the ocean, the cardinal on your neighbor's railing, the Angel Trumpet flower in the yard below. Take in every image as a touch of Me, and whenever you use your lips, know I am with you in every thought and every word. We are One. *HS, I still feel an excitement about my "end of life celebration" and the relief of knowing it will happen, even if the world has blown up by then. Nothing can spoil it. It is out of my hands and You will take charge. This is a joyful state of mind.*

137

One in Love

It is your love of Me, of God,
that calls to the heart of the brother.

May 9, 2021

We are One. There is nowhere to go and nothing to do. Your friend April has strayed like a lost sheep from My Fold. I will use your love of Me to bring her back. Yes, that is the way to see every encounter. It is your love of Me, of God, that calls to their heart and enfolds them in My Grace. You don't ever need to work on acceptance or love of another entity as a dream character. When you love Me, then you love My "creation"—the extension of all the many selves made up in the mind. We are One in Love and all the world is in our Heart; United. This is how your Identification as One with God is extended into the "world of dreams." There are no specifics, no people, no world. It is One Self that embraces all Life.

Thank You, Holy Spirit. This is beautiful and I get it in a new way. There is no separation or judgment when my focus is Only on You and Our Identity as One with God. In this way, I am always looking past the world to You, the One Who encompasses all. Symbolically, I ate my self, my projection, this Mother's Day when I consumed the empty womb of a papaya with two tiny "babies." Now we are incorporated into One. That was the perfect symbol for this morning. You are showing your willingness to ingest the entire dream of separation and make it yours—One with God.

138

Mystery Solved

It is My Energy that sets the blueprint of the Universe.

July 17, 2021

Holy Spirit, speak to me of the morning. We wrote together about your symbolic encounter with the Tree of Life—the pink Tacoma tree at the corner of your building, which was covered with birds . . . pink and gray Java sparrows, mynahs, doves, finches, cardinals, and a Japanese white eye. You watched the sparrows gather in groups repeatedly rearranging themselves on different branches over the twenty minutes you were there. Then, they would fly off alone, or in pairs, or groups of three, four, five, covering the four directions.

What is their constant reorganization about before they fly? They await My command. It is inherent. The call for every movement comes from Me. That is also the way of the planets and humanity. My pattern is set along with My timing for everything to fall into place. The birds, the fractals, kaleidoscope patterns, stones on the beach, all move as directed. The birds do not plan. I am the Planner. Nothing is haphazard or happenstance. It is My Energy that sets the blueprint of the Universe; the collapse of stars, the storms, the wars, the rising and falling of civilizations. I hold the strings of the Dancing Universe; everything in its perfect place in a perfect dream. Yes, your progression Home is clearly in My Hands. The dream contains "probability" and that is also under My control. The awakening is planned for each, like the timing for a bird to hop off a branch. Nature demonstrates the creation and extension of the Christ of God.

You now see and sense My Constancy behind what appears as a chaotic world. It is not in chaos and has a purpose. It must be taken as a whole. Even iron filings know their place through My delineation. I am the Master Craftsman/Artist. All is Masterminded by Me. Nothing escapes My Script, My Plan. You, as a tiny cell, are in your sector coming together with your many groupings over lifetimes, fulfilling your mission in each foray until the tree of life is bare, all missions completed, and you are Home. This is what you saw reflected by the birds today . . . leaving, and then returning regrouped. Some took their final leave for the day/lifetime, but all were being called to meet at this time and in that tree to complete the manifestation of a Sacred Plan. *HS, I see all the people in my life as groups of sparrows or mynah birds leaving Home to forage on their own. Raise me above the dream to see the Big Design with You.* You have released to Me the last elements of your commitment to each phase of your life, and now you See without the veils of attachment to the allurement of and attraction to form.

Tonight, near the pink Tacoma tree, you watched the setting of the full harvest moon. The fruit is ready to fall from the tree. This is the puzzle on the universal level, solved—you are a particle in the out picture, but in reality, you are Me—the Creator. That is the Mystery. *HS, is that the meaning of "Big and Little"— a phrase that often popped into my mind as a child? It always left me with the feeling of having overwhelming importance, but made no sense.* Yes, you are *sooo* Big you can't conceive of your apparent littleness. *And vice versa?* Yes. It cannot be reconciled without Knowing Me, My Voice, and My Knowledge. This is the solution to the *big* and *little* conundrum that came into your child mind, which made no sense and tormented you. The projected image mt does not have the capacity to know or understand the Immensity of her Beingness as One with God, but because your decision maker knows you are the dreamer of a dream, it gets it—our Connection is Infinite. *I am Big and Little . . . mt is little, but my Self is Big—All that Is. Thank You, HS.*

139

Awake

Every aspect of the world reflects your own stage of awakening.

September 17, 2021

What are You, Holy Spirit? I am not an entity inside of you, in your brain, or in your mind. I Am *you.* We can never be severed; never split. You, as a character, do not exist other than as an idea. You are the projector of this world, "born" of a passing thought that you left Home. The world will be washed away. It's only been a dream. We are One Self "walking the world" awake. There was no sleep. No separation. The dream is over. You have awakened to it. Our Unity has never been gone. The God Mind, which you are, has never been assailed. Nothing can attack your Invulnerability. Only the Truth/Light of our Being exists. The tiny mad idea has no meaning for you now. Nothing of a dream can ever be real. We Are One. We are Home.

Every aspect of the world reflects your own stage of awakening, and all must awaken from their lie of a dream separate from their Self/God/Me. For you, there is nowhere else to go and nothing more to do. Just continue the tasks that were set up in the beginning of time, knowing we only review a completed dream script. Even if the ego tries to intervene, you now have the Knowledge that you were the "dreamer" of a dream that is long over and Done. You, the Self, are One with God.

From Kenneth Wapnick, Ph.D, "You know that you are right near the end of the journey when you recognize there is no voice for God. You're the voice for God. There is only one voice in your right mind. It's not Jesus, it's not the Holy Spirit's, it's not yours by the name you think of yourself as being. It's the one Voice that's everyone's Voice. We all, not only have that voice, we ARE that voice." (*Joy of Learning; Chapter 1.*)

Afterword

Holy Spirit, what do You say now?

You, Jo, and Meera have completed your Mission in this and all lifetimes—to become United as One with God; witnessed in My series of the seven *OWG* books. You have shared the process of your awakening from this dream world through daily communication of My messages to each of you. By deepening your commitment to ask Me about every aspect of your lives, you have come to know, depend upon, and trust Me implicitly. This is a big order, and it was accomplished through your ever-expanding willingness to follow My present and available Guidance.

Over time you have relinquished all earthly attachment to ego roles and beliefs, including special relationships with family, friends, and acquaintances. As I became the only Informer of your lives, you experienced My Constancy and Peace in the midst of every worldly upset, conundrum, and challenge. You each clearly experience being "lived and spoken" by Me. Nothing has been too much or too little to illicit My Loving attention and instruction. You also have witnessed a growing kindness in your personal interactions, while staying detached from any ego expectations to take responsibility for another's situation. You have seen the world and all the many selves as just the projection of your own identification with the suffering caused by the belief in separation. You now know your Reality is in the Mind of God and that your dream character has no value other than performing My Will.

We conclude knowing that you have accomplished the exhortation given at the conclusion of the Workbook in *A Course in Miracles* to hear but the Voice for God and Awaken from the dream of separation. Your work is finished, although you will complete any final tasks under My auspices. Each reader will be given their next step tailored to their own Divine trajectory. The very last step will be taken as God lifts you into Unity—Oneness with Him.

Amen.

CPSIA information can be obtained
at www.ICGtesting.com
Printed in the USA
LVHW021735211221
706851LV00012B/576

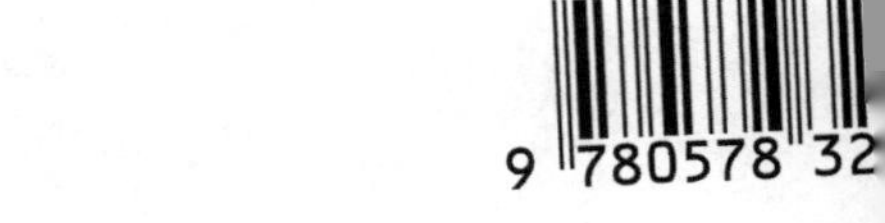